THE
BATT

ADAM
WEBB

DIB DOB
DEB DEB

Other gamebooks available in Armada

The Grailquest series
The Castle of Darkness
The Den of Dragons
The Gateway of Doom
Voyage of Terror
Kingdom of Horror
Realm of Chaos
Tomb of Nightmares
Legion of the Dead

The Monster Horrorshow

Dracula's Castle
The Curse of Frankenstein

J. H. Brennan

Earthbrain

Keith Faulkner

Dragonquest

David Hill

The Puzzlequest series
The Great Spy Race
The Riddle of the Sphinx

Michael Holt

The Duelmaster series
Challenge of the Magi
Blood Valley
The Shattered Realm
Arena of Death

Mark Smith and Jamie Thomson

THE LAST BATTLEDROID

Maldraggon and the Droid Master

With the echoes of the emergency alert siren still ringing around the chipped-granite walls of the Museum of Ancient Works and Technology, you, the recently appointed assistant curator, hurriedly enter your viewing room. The holographic screen before you bursts into life, creating a three-dimensional image of the Holy Emperor Vizo Rath, the ruler of your galaxy for the past 140 years. His face looks haggard and drawn as he begins his public address . . .

"Citizens of Anthracitex-9, as your elected guardian and spokesman, it is my sad duty to reveal to you the tragic news which we have just decoded from our probe-satellite, Pilgrim VII. As you all know, your planet and her neighbours in the Caluphex Galaxy have been at peace for over thirty decades, since the terrible Droid Wars of 3050 A.D. In that fateful year, we proudly conquered the vast battlefleets of the Fentusian General Maldraggon, and immobilised his Flag-Automaton, plucking him alive from its belly.

"Yet we did not, in our anger, seek to destroy this foul master of destruction. My predecessor, General Voril-Rath, instead deemed it wise to spare his life as an example of the power of good over evil, a twisted symbol of the peace. Maldraggon was frozen alive, his body sealed in a transparent capsule of argonite, preserved but effectively neutralised. The capsule was jettisoned into deepest Space and set on an orbital path to pass through our galaxy once every eleven years. His twisted body and tortured gaze have served as a ghastly reminder, for successive generations, of the terrible power of evil.

"Furthermore, your forefathers, in their infinite wisdom, attempted to establish a lasting peace by ridding our system of every conceivable engine of war. All our planet's armaments, and those of our Caluphexian neighbours, were vapourised, cleansing our galaxy yet leaving it naked and defenceless. After 308 years of tranquility, our experiment in peace has gone terribly wrong . . .

"At this year's massive celebrations to mark the 28th 'Orbit of Maldraggon', we failed to sight his argonite capsule. Alarmed, we despatched Pilgrim VII on a data-collection mission to the fringes of the Fentusian Galaxy. Its sensors detected a previously unrecorded energy source deep in the core of the galaxy, and traced it to a huge, artificial planet. Pilgrim VII flew in to close orbit and transmitted the following information:

"'The artificial planet Mirestar, 2000 kilometres in circumference and densely populated, emits an energy level of 3.8 million joules. Techno-scans reveal a technical factor of twelve, seven points higher than Anthracitex-9. Micro-tech scan registers highly powerful weapon sources; advanced droid and automaton development, photon-pulse and laser weaponry, and over 100 force-shielded craft with lightspeed capability.'

"Our presence must have been detected during scanning, for the following message was transmitted to our probe:

"'As if from death, I, Maldraggon, have arisen. The centuries that I drifted in suspension have not been wasted, for while my body was locked in argonite, my brain was thinking but one thought: revenge on all the people of Caluphex. I have no need for surprise. You have sealed your own fate, and can only await my triumphant return . . .'

"As you are all aware, my people, we have no means of repelling invaders. By our computer's calculations, Maldraggon's dark forces will fly unchallenged into our galaxy within twenty-one days. Already, his mighty hand has cast probes and mutant-spores throughout the galaxies to spread his evil terror, in preparation for the final assault. In the interests of preventing unnecessary bloodshed, I ask you to await with dignity our inevitable conquest. The Inter-Planetary Rockworm Police have been ordered to arrest anyone making unauthorised space travel.

"I will broadcast further bulletins every six hours, until Maldraggon assumes the presidency. I can only express my infinite regret..."

As you stare at the screen in disbelief, the hologram slowly fades away. The thought that a loathsome creature such as the infamous Maldraggon can, unchallenged, take over your planet and your life reviles you, and very slowly a strange idea begins to form in your mind.

The museum in which you now stand is the only place in the galaxy where weapons are still to be seen, and you are one of very few people with the knowledge and skill to use them. Your many years of apprenticeship were spent studying the weapon guidance-systems and laser defence-shields of the great battle robots, and examining the complex training manuals used by the droid pilots so many years ago. Now is the time to put your study to good use.

With a pounding heart, you rush into the deserted main gallery. Towering high above the hundreds of carefully restored machines, relics of a bygone age, stands the museum's greatest exhibit, the 200-metre tall Samurai-Class Battledroid. Stepping up to the central security console, you pass your hand over the bio-reader, automatically locking all the museum's entrances and exits. Then, just as you did when you were a small child, you activate the infospeak panel...

"This Samurai-Class Battledroid was designed and built by the Tamil-Rath Droid Masters in 3048 A.D. The Battledroid was the mainstay of the Caluphexian defences during the 3050 A.D. Droid Wars, but has since been rendered obsolete by the cybernetic developments of distant galaxies. Designed primarily as a 'terranean droid', it is incapable of light-speed space-flight, and its highly explosive laser-banks require regular recharging. It is, though, a highly versatile machine, equipped with extensive attack, defence, and work facilities. Because of its incredible size and power, the Battledroid would, if skilfully piloted, make a formidable opponent even for today's highly-advanced droids."

After listening to these familiar words, you step across to the facility-loader console and begin to select the weapon, work and defence systems that you feel will best suit your mission to conquer Maldraggon.

Specifications

Due to its great age, the Battledroid may not operate at its full capacity. You must roll dice to determine its condition, and fill in the results on the Status Chart at the beginning of the book.

1. Roll one dice and add 12 to the score. Fill in the total in the space marked ATTACK CAPACITY. This number represents the Battledroid's attacking strength.
2. Roll one dice and add 6 to the score. Fill in the total in the space marked DEFENCE CAPACITY. This number represents the strength of the Battledroid's outer shields.
3. Roll 2 dice and add 20 to the score. Fill in the total in the space marked MAXIMUM, and shade in the same number of squares representing the Battledroid's laser-banks. This number represents the Battledroid's power, and will go down when you are damaged in battle or when the Battledroid uses large amounts of energy. When you lose some laser-reserves, rub out the appropriate number of squares. When you are told that you may recharge your laser-banks, shade in the squares up to their initial maximum again. If the Battledroid's laser-banks ever equal 0, you have failed your quest.

4. When you recharge the Battledroid, both attack capacity and defence capacity, and all missile charges will rise back to their initial value. They may only exceed their initial value when specifically instructed.
5. Roll two dice and write the score in the space marked COMPUTER CAPACITY. This number represents the amount of information held in the Battledroid's computer banks, and as your quest continues, it may rise or fall from its initial value.
6. The number 7 in the space marked PILOT SKILL represents your ability to pilot the Battledroid and may rise above its initial value as your adventure proceeds.
7. The space marked TIME is for you to record how many days have passed in your mission. When you are instructed to add on time, shade in a square for each day. The higher this number is, the more danger there will be of encountering Maldraggon's armies.
8. Also marked on your Status Chart is your LIFE FORCE, which measures your own health and is rated at 7 at the start of the adventure. If you are injured while piloting the Battledroid, you will be instructed to reduce your life force value. If your life force ever reaches 0, you have failed in your mission.

Equipping the Battledroid

The diagrams of the front and back of the Battledroid (Figs. 1 & 2) are labelled with the numbers of facility-holders. These correspond to the numbered facilities available for use with the Battledroid (Fig. 3).

There are far more facilities available for use with the Battledroid than it can carry at one time. You must select from the facilities described on the following pages those which you think will be most helpful to your mission.

The Battledroid is capable of carrying a maximum load of 60 tonnes. It is up to you to equip it with as many facilities as possible without exceeding this maximum payload. If you choose too many items, you must remove as many as is necessary to reduce the total weight to 60 tonnes or less. Only then will the Battledroid become capable of movement.

When you choose a facility, write down its name, facility number, type and weight on the Status Chart. You will find your mission most successful if you choose facilities from all 3 categories:

A: Defence Facilities (2–12)

The numbers 2–12 shown in circles on the Battledroid diagrams (Figs. 1 and 2) represent the random hit areas of the Battledroid. The matching defence facilities which protect these areas are numbered 2–12 on Fig. 3. All these defence facilities extend to the rear of the Battledroid. You must only, though, note down the facility once on your Status Chart.

The defence facilities represent the Battledroid's final defences after its outer shields are penetrated. When an enemy scores a successful hit against you in combat, from either front or rear, you must roll two dice to determine which area of the Battledroid has been damaged. If you have a defence facility in this area, it absorbs damage up to its maximum absorption. If you don't have the defence facility for this area, then full damage is deducted from your laser-banks.

—When a defence facility absorbs damage, it is not harmed in any way. Its absorption remains the same throughout combat, and throughout your quest.
—The defence facility is weaker at the rear, and its maximum absorption when you are attacked from behind is halved. E.g. A droid scores 8 points of damage on the Battledroid.

The player rolls two dice, and scores 4. The Battledroid has been struck in area 4, the left shoulder:
—If the player does not have Facility 4 he deducts 8 points from his laser reserves.
—If the player does have Facility 4, Laserite Deflector, and the droid was attacking from the front, the Battledroid absorbs 6 points of damage. Only 2 points are deducted from the laser reserves.
—If the player does have Facility 4, but the droid attacked from the rear, the Battledroid absorbs 3 points of damage. 5 points are deducted from the laser reserves.

There is no defence facility available for area 7. If the Battledroid is struck in this area, full damage is deducted from its laser-banks. The Battledroid's most vulnerable areas, as you will see later, are its internal electronics (area 7) and its control turret (area 2), both of which may cause malfunctions when damaged.

B: Attack Facilities (13–20)

The numbers of the attack facilities (Figs. 1 and 3) and their facility-holders (Fig. 1) are shown in squares. While the facilities are all shown on the front diagram (Fig. 1), the attack facilities may also be used against an enemy attacking from the rear. When you choose an attack facility, note its name, facility number, weight, range, type, charges and bonus on your Status Chart.

—An attack facility's bonus may be added to your combat score in certain encounters. When you enter combat with an enemy, you will be told which attack facilities gain their bonus, and which attack facilities cannot be used. If you have a facility which is not specified, you may still use it, but it gains no bonus. An attack facility may only be used when the enemy is within its minimum and maximum range.

—Some attack facilities will be able to use their bonus more often, while others have a greater bonus. It is important to choose a wide selection of attack facilities, for if you meet an opponent who is invulnerable to all your attack facilities, your quest will be at an end.

—If you choose a Missile attack facility, note down the number of charges it has on your Status Chart. Every combat round you fire the facility, deduct one charge. When you have no charges left, the facility is exhausted and may not be used. You may, though, place all charges back on maximum when you recharge the Battledroid's laser-banks.

C: Work Facilities (21–28)

The numbers of the work facilities (Figs. 2 and 3) are shown in diamonds. When you choose a work facility, note its name, facility number and weight on the Status Chart.

The work facilities are designed for the various utility tasks which the Battledroid performs. They can be used in the quest where specified, and may prove vital at certain points to the continuation of your mission.

—The Watchdog Missile Guidance System may only be used with Missile attack facilities.

The Battledroid has the following facilities available:

A: Defence Facilities
(Absorption shows rear-absorption in brackets)

2. *Laser-Intercept Helm*: (Weight = 4) (Absorption = 6(3))
   A laserite-armour helm equipped with heat-sensitive lasers to intercept attacks to the Battledroid's head. The

control turret is one of the most important areas to defend.

3. *Laserite Deflector*: (Weight = 4) (Absorption = 6(3))
   A laser-impregnated plate designed to reflect attacks from the Battledroid's right shoulder, producing a shimmering blue force-field.

4. *Laserite Deflector*: (Weight = 4) (Absorption = 6(3))
   A laser-impregnated plate designed to deflect attacks from the Battledroid's left shoulder, producing a shimmering blue force-field.

5. *Magno-Plates*: (Weight = 2) (Absorption = 4(2))
   Electrically-charged armour generating a magnetic force-field capable of deflecting and absorbing laser fire.

6. *Magno-Plates*: (Weight = 2) (Absorption = 4(2))
   Electrically-charged armour generating a magnetic force-field capable of deflecting and absorbing laser fire.

7. *Internal Electronics*: There is no defence facility available for this area. Any damage in this area has full effect and may cause malfunctions.

8. *Tuskquartz Energy Globe*: (Weight = 4) (Absorption = 6(3))
   Armour crafted from the precious Tuskquartz mineral, capable of absorbing high levels of energy.

9. *Photonite Shielding*: (Weight = 3) (Absorption = 4(2))
   Photonite plating covered with a highly-charged flickering red proton force-field, defending Battledroid's right-lower torso.

10. *Photonite Shielding*: (Weight = 3) (Absorption = 4(2))
    Photonite plating covered with a highly-charged flickering red proton force-field defending Battledroid's left-lower torso.

11. *Laserite Interceptor*: (Weight = 1) (Absorption = 2(1))
    Laserite armour automatically concentrating defensive bursts of blinding white laser energy in exact area of attack. Defends right-leg machinery.

12. *Laserite Interceptor*: (Weight = 1) (Absorption = 2(1))
    Laserite armour automatically concentrating defensive bursts of blinding white laser energy in exact area of attack. Defends left-leg machinery.

B: Attack Facilities
(A weapon with infinite charges (INF) may be used as many times as desired.)

13. *Rotary Laser-bomb Launcher*: (Weight = 5)
    (Range = 0–3km) (Type = MISSILE) (Charges = 5)
    (Bonus = 3)
    A rapidly-revolving device launching 50 explosive, high-velocity laser-bombs for each charge. Used on few modern droids.

14. *Psi-Exuder*: (Weight = 5) (Range = 0–1km)
    (Type = TECHNOLOGICAL) (Charges = INF.)
    (Bonus = 2)
    A powerful transmitter which invades the body-cells of living organisms and the electronics of droids, through the rapid emission of shock-waves generated by the pilot's own life-force. Although banned by the modern guild of droid-builders, because of its unknown effect on the health of pilots, it remains a very effective weapon.

15. *Laser Port*: (Weight = 7) (Range = 0–5km)
    (Type = MISSILE) (Charges = 8) (Bonus = 4)
    An immensely powerful weapon which fires a scorching laser beam; standard fitting on most modern combat-droids.

16. *Sonic Punch*: (Weight = 7) (Range = 0–250m)
    (Type = CLOSE COMBAT) (Charges = INF.)
    (Bonus = 3)
    A compressed-air extending laserite battering-ram, releasing a sonic explosion upon impact, designed to fend off opponents and punch through armour. The Sonic Punch can sometimes be used jointly with other weapons, and may double as a work facility for pounding and drilling through rock.

17. *Negative-Ion Flame Thrower*: (Weight = 6)
    (Range = 0–2km) (Type = MISSILE) (Charges = 6)
    (Bonus = 4)
    A high-pressure jet-cannon which simultaneously releases and ignites a cone of hydrogen, capable of melting flesh, piercing certain force-fields and igniting laser-banks.

18. *Nuclear Gas/Water/Radiation Jet*: (Weight = 6)
    (Range = 0–1km) (Type = CLOSE COMBAT)
    (Charges = INF.) (Bonus = 4)
    A photon-powered jet-cannon which can release either a thin jet or a wide spray of toxic gas, water or radiation with lethal force. This facility was designed to comabt large humanoid forces, and proved very effective on the planet Jethal in dispersing the Mutant Riots of 3049 A.D.

19. *Heat-Seeking Atomic Torpedo Launcher*: (Weight = 7)
    (Range = 3–20km) (Type = TECHNOLOGICAL)
    (Charges = 3) (Bonus = 5)

A launching-pod highly charged with laser energy, designed to propel heat-seeking torpedoes over great distances with high accuracy. This facility can be used for either bombarding towns, creating a devastating explosion and widespread radiation, or long-range combat with large droids. Note that it cannot be used against an opponent closer than 2km.

20. *Tail-Guard Disintegrator*: (Weight = 5) (Range = 0–2km) (Type = MISSILE) (Charges = 6) (Bonus = 4)

    A computer-guided laser port which emits rays capable of disrupting molecular structure, so reducing opponents to dust. This weapon may only be used against enemies to the rear, but in doing so automatically gains its bonus; unless the enemy is immune to this facility.

C: Work Facilities

21. *Satellite-Informed Radar Scan*: (Weight = 3)

    A sensitive radar, linked to the information satellites scattered throughout the galaxies. It can scan entire planets, registering life-forms and techno-factors, or investigate smaller areas and map them on the Battledroid's 3-D viewing-disc.

22. *Watchdog Missile Guidance System*: (Weight = 4)

    This facility gives heat-seeking, computer-linked targeting and magnetic-tracing qualities to any missile fired by the Battledroid. If you choose this facility, add 2 to your initial attack capacity whenever you are using a MISSILE attack facility.

23. *Gamma-Wave Intercom*: (Weight = 3)

    A transmitter connected to a holographic screen and cameras. This facility is necessary to send and receive detailed communications while in the Battledroid's control turret.

24. *Automated Claw*: (Weight = 5)
A highly-advanced facility capable of grasping any object with minimal pressure, or crushing it to pulp.

25. *Auxiliary Oxygen Supply*: (Weight = 5)
A high-technology globe which converts the Battledroid's fuel-waste into oxygen, allowing life-support systems to continue functioning when the Battledroid's standard air-filters are unable to operate.

26. *Mutant Sensory Unit*: (Weight = 4)
This device, grown from the living spores of mutants, relays what it sees around it to the Battledroid's Visual Display Units. The computer can then analyse important data and create, if required, three-dimensional replicas for the pilot to see, hear, smell, taste and touch.

27. *Manually-Operated Shuttle*: (Weight = 6)
Armed, lightweight one-man capsule designed for use where the Battledroid's size renders it inoperative. Using an advanced computer-link, the shuttle fights at the same attack, defence and laser-bank capacities as the Battledroid. This does mean, though, that any damage inflicted upon the shuttle will drain the normal amount of power from the Battledroid's laser banks, and if the shuttle is destroyed while in operation, so the Battledroid will also be destroyed. The shuttle has no defence facilities to absorb damage, and must fight combat with its laser-port (Bonus = 0) (Range = 0–1km) (Charges = INF.). It is also equipped with a micro-computer and a simple grab. The shuttle can travel up to 5km from the Battledroid.

28. *Independent Information Probe*: (Weight = 5)
    A micro-chip operated globe armed with a miniature automated claw and special sensory feelers. It can be despatched independently up to its maximum range of 7km, to return information to you via the Battledroid's computer.

When you have selected your facilities and noted their details on your Status Chart, add up their total weight in tonnes and write it in the space provided. If this number is above 60 tonnes you must remove or exchange some facilities. If it is equal to or below 60 tonnes, your Battledroid is ready to move.

Movement

The Battledroid you are about to pilot has four different modes of movement:
1. SPACE – which must only be used when the Battledroid is travelling through Space at sub-light speed along the interplanetary ley-lines.
2. STRIDE – which moves the Battledroid across land by simulated leg movements.
3. HOVER – which raises and propels the Battledroid by means of anti-gravity, electron-pulse jets, using up small amounts of laser-bank energy.
4. TRACKS – which propels the Battledroid over land or through water by means of Tuskquartz powered caterpillar-tracks.

On your Status Chart are two circles under the heading of movement. The first circle shows you which quarter represents which mode of movement. You must shade in the quarter of the second circle which represents the movement you are using. If you wish to change your mode of movement at the end of a section, simply rub out one quarter and shade in another.

Combat

When you are forced or choose to fight an enemy, note down the Battledroid's and the opponent's specifications on the Battle Chart. When you sustain any damage, make the necessary adjustments to your laser reserves on the Status Chart. Do not forget to deduct charges when using attack facilities which require them.

Use the following system for combat:–

1. Unless you are told otherwise, your opponent attacks first, and you must proceed from stage 2. If you are instructed to attack first, proceed from stage 10.

2. Roll two dice and add the score to your opponent's attack capacity, to give his ATTACK SCORE.

3. Roll two dice and add the score to your defence capacity, to give your DEFENCE SCORE.

4. If your defence score is higher than or equal to your opponent's attack score, his attack has been absorbed by the Battledroid's outer defence shields. No damage is done, and you may begin your own attack at stage 10.

5. If your defence score is lower than your opponent's attack score, the Battledroid has been hit. Subtract your defence score from his attack score to give the DAMAGE TOTAL.

6. Roll two dice to score a number between 2 and 12, and find the corresponding number on the Battledroid diagram, to determine where you have been hit. (Check Fig. 1 if you are being attacked from the front, and Fig. 2 if you are being attacked from the rear. All attacks come from the front unless stated otherwise.). If you have a defence facility in this area, deduct its absorption from the damage total. (Remember that the absorption is halved if the attack comes from the rear.) Any remaining damage is

deducted from your laser-banks. If your defence facility's absorption is higher than the damage total, no actual damage has been done.

If you do not have a defence facility in the area hit, deduct the full damage total from your laser reserves.

7. If you have sustained any actual damage in the Battledroid's control tower (area 2) make a note of the total damage sustained there.

8. If you have sustained any damage in the Battledroid's internal electronics (area 7), note down the total damage sustained there.

9. If your laser-banks fall to zero, then the Battledroid has been destroyed, and you have failed in your mission.

10. If your Battledroid is still functioning, you can now launch an attack. First, select an attack facility, making sure that your enemy is within its range. (If your opponent is immune to all your weapons, you have failed your mission).

    Roll two dice and add the total to the Battledroid's attack capacity, to give your ATTACK SCORE.
    – If you are instructed to, add the bonus for the attack facility.
    – If the facility is not specified, you may still use it, but it gains no bonus.
    – If your enemy is attacking from the rear, you may add the bonus if you are using a Tail-Guard Disintegrator.
    – Add 2 if you are using a Missile weapon and have a Watchdog Missile Guidance System.

11. Roll two dice and add the total to your opponent's defence capacity, to give his DEFENCE SCORE.

12. If your attack score is lower than or equal to your opponent's defence score, your attack has failed: go back to stage 2, and begin a new combat round.

13. If your attack score is higher than your opponent's defence score, you have penetrated his outer shields. Subtract his defence score from your attack score to establish the DAMAGE TOTAL.

14. Deduct your opponent's absorption from the damage total, and subtract the result from his laser or life reserves. If his shield absorption is higher than your damage total, no actual damage has been done.

    If you have reduced your opponent's laser or life reserves to zero you have destroyed him: go to stage 15. If you have not, begin a new combat round from stage 2.

15. If the Battledroid's control turret (area 2) has been damaged, note down the encounter number and turn to **321**, to check for potential malfunctions and pilot injury.

16. If the Battledroid's internal electronics (area 7) have been damaged, note down the encounter number and turn to **322**, to check for potential malfunction.

When you are fighting from the Manually-Operated Shuttle, follow the above combat system. The shuttle has the same capacities as the Battledroid and runs off its laser-banks. You gain no facility bonus for the Shuttle since its laser port (Bonus = 0) is its only attack facility. There is no need to determine where the Shuttle has been damaged since it has no defence facilities, and full damage is automatically deducted from the Battledroid's laser-banks.

Maldraggon and the Droid Master

The Quest

Stepping back from the computerised facility-loader, you gaze up in awe at the fully-equipped Battledroid. Only time will tell whether or not you have equipped it with the systems required to complete your quest.

Drawing a Molecular Disruptor from its holster on a neighbouring exhibit, you stride towards the entry hatch in one of the Battledroid's massive tracked feet. You slip your hand into the bio-sensor, and the hatch slides open with a hiss. Inside the air-lock, you step into the elevator pod, and as you ascend you begin to ponder on the recklessness of your actions. While you have studied the workings of the Battledroid in great depth, you have never actually piloted the immense machine. The voyage ahead will certainly be one of discovery . . .

Brushing aside any thoughts of abandoning your perilous quest, you begin to formulate a plan of campaign. Realising that it would be suicidal to head straight for Mirestar, you resolve to seek out the person capable of offering you some hope of success in the coming conflict. As the elevator pod slows to a halt, you recall the legends you heard as a child of the great Tamil-Rath Droid Masters. The Droid Masters were the hereditary line of brilliant cybernetic engineers who developed and built the Battledroids, but whose services became unnecessary when the galaxy disarmed in 3050 A.D.

This proud bloodline, renowned for their unpredictable genius, chose self-imposed exile rather than face the prospect of a world without their beloved droids. Without warning, they suddenly abandoned their own planet, Ironis-2. Piloting fantastic droids designed after the symbol of the Droid Masters – a globe within a blazing circle, through which they were said to have discovered the secret of eternal motion – they fled to distant galaxies.

The voyage of the Droid Masters was not well-blessed. Some say that they carried with them the heavy burden of a curse cast from the foul lips of Maldraggon as the argonite capsule embraced him. One by one, the ill-fated Droid Masters met untimely deaths. Only the fate of Gan Tamil-Rath remains uncertain. Legend tells that he piloted his strange craft into the swirling mists of the Fentusian Gulf, a poorly charted region between Caluphex and Fentusia. Landing on Oric, a tiny crimson planet of smouldering lava, he sought to befriend its strange and hostile inhabitants. Gan Tamil-Rath has never been seen since. Some, though, say that he grows old at the heart of the planet, madness casting a sinister shade over his solitary genius, as he continues his ancestors' quest for cybernetic perfection. If the myths are to be believed, your mission lies on Oric, with the Last of the Droid Masters.

You emerge from your ascent into the dimly lit control centre, and slide into the pilot's couch, which vibrates as it reforms to match your body contours. The word 'identify' appears on the computer screen, and you slip your hand into the bio-sensor. Instantly, a voice identical to your own announces, 'Welcome aboard! This is Samurai Class Battledroid SB246, awaiting your command. You are cleared for pilot control. Please proceed.' As you pass your hand over the master power-pad, there is a distant hum and suddenly the control centre is bathed in light. Dust billows into the turret as the air-filters burst into life, and replace the stale, musty atmosphere with fresh, clean air. The turret rocks slightly as its gyro-sensors adjust to your additional weight. Banks of info-panels glow a dull red around you and liquid crystal displays rise to their maximum levels. The blast shutters that encircle the Battledroid's head slide smoothly up into their recesses, revealing the 360°-vision laser-impregnated glass screen. You run the systems check program which confirms that all systems are fully operational. An eerie luminous blue glow surrounds the Battledroid as its standard defence shields reach maximum power. With this magnificent droid at your command, you suddenly feel that you are capable of fulfilling your mission.

Your first problem is to commandeer a light-speed Space Trucker to carry the Battledroid to the planet Oric in the Fentusian Gulf in time. The Battledroid's electron-pulse engines simply don't have the speed to make the journey before Maldraggon's evil host engulfs your galaxy. You must head for the SpaceDrome, 20 kilometres to the north. Your Craft Master from the museum is currently studying there and he would be sure to help you.

While there is nothing on Anthracitex-9 capable of standing against the 200-metre high Battledroid, you must avoid any possibility of endangering your own people in your quest to save the galaxy. At your word of command, 'Hover', you feel the droid begin to rise, powered by its long dormant engines, a tribute to the great skill of the Droid Masters. The speed of ascent increases, until, with a deafening crash, the Battledroid emerges through the domed glass roof of the museum . . . Turn to **1**.

1

Blue flames shoot from the Battledroid's huge hover jets, as you rise slowly up into the blustery atmosphere which cloaks Anthracitex-9's landscape of granite cliffs. Many small craft, known as Hover-Bugs, blast streams of crimson dust down from their anti-gravity jets as they skim along several metres above the broad passes that cut through the black rock. Shimmering blue electric force-gates, blocking the roads, are manned by their guards: enormous, heavily-armoured creatures known as Rockworms, who make up the Inter-Galactic Police. These 500-kilogramme giants, known more for their brutality than their intelligence, press their short, grey, scaly-skinned arms against flickering control panels to lower the force-fields and allow travellers carrying Travel Crystals to pass. They turn any unauthorized travellers back, flourishing 3-metre stun rods at their Hover-Bugs.

The granite peaks and the neon-blue force-gates rise up into the scarlet-tinged cloud which always hangs over your planet. In ancient times, criminals were jettisoned into this strange mist, and as a child you were always strictly ordered to fly your Space Podule well below it.

If you wish to guide the Battledroid down on to the granite roadway beneath the museum, turn to **271**.

If you wish to thrust the Battledroid up into the scarlet vapour, turn to **87**.

2

You travel for three kilometres, the distress signal growing clearer as you near it, until finally the viewing screen reveals its source. A 40-metre tall robot, consisting primarily of two gangling metal legs, is sprinting around a steel spike, to which it is tethered. Strapped to the top of the robot is a captured Caluphexian Distress-Beacon. It is a trap!

A Fentusian Fire-Fly, a tiny but lethal piloted droid, rises up out of a smoking mound behind the robot. It lowers its attack facilities and launches a huge heat-seeking missile. With a drone the missile soars towards you.

If you wish to switch off the Battledroid's master switch, to deactivate the Battledroid, turn to **261**.

If you wish to prime your attack facilities against the Fentusian Fire-Fly, turn to **155**.

3

The limping craft unleashes a round of heavy fire at the Battledroid, and an assortment of sharpened metal objects, including some rather exquisite bronze statuettes, pepper your defence shields. You have no choice but to enter combat. (Range = 1km)

If you have, and wish to use, a Negative-Ion Flame Thrower, turn to **135**.

MERCENARY SPACE-SHUTTLE: Attack = 8 Defence = 4 Absorption = 1 Laser Reserves = 5 (Gain Bonus for Laser Port) (Immune to Nuclear Jet)

If you defeat the Mercenary, turn to **163**.

4

The Black Widow Spider Droid explodes and plummets down to Oric's crimson surface. Your celebrations, though, are halted by the sudden silence of your computer-simulation of Holy Emperor Vizo Rath's heartbeat. Your computers indicate that the Overseer of your galaxy died in the same instant as the defeated Spider Droid plunged into the lava-pools of Oric. Without Vizo Rath's guidance, your galaxy remains at the mercy of the Fentusian hordes. You have failed in your mission.

5

Suddenly a huge Flesh Mutant slithers into the chamber, using its four claws to drag along its bloated belly. Its snaking tail trails back into the tubeway. Growing in strength with every victim it claims, the Flesh Mutant springs towards you, flourishing a Laser Whip. (Range = 200m)

FLESH MUTANT: Attack = 10 Defence = 7 Absorption = 2 Life Reserves = 20 (Gain Bonus for Laser Port) (Immune to Rotary Laser-Bomb Launcher)

If you win, turn to **116**.

6

Using vocal commands you guide the Automated Claw down on to the mercury-disc, its piston puffing, its motors moaning.

The Claw presses down on the silver dias, to no effect, and as it tries to grasp the smooth surface, its steel-link fingers scrabble and scrape without finding a grip. The Claw clatters against the glass and its sharp fingers screech over the surface, creating enough noise to disturb something high in the cavern.

A Flame Drake launches a screaming droid, shaped like the Pterodactyls you once studied in Primitive History of Flight classes, which swoops down from its roost towards you, laser ports blazing. It attacks from the rear. (Range = 500m)

> FLAME DRAKE PTEROPOD: Attack = 13 Defence = 9 Absorption = 1 Laser Reserves = 12 (Gain Bonus for Laser Port) (Immune to Nuclear Jet)

If you defeat the Pteropod, turn to **150**.

7

The Battledroid strides out across the light-bridge as it retracts towards you. There are 300 metres left to travel, and the light-bridge is receding at 10 metres per second. You are powering along at 30 metres per second, and must program a leap into the Battledroid's stride-pattern, to clear the gulf across to the Space Hangar's central platform, at the last possible moment.

If you wish the Battledroid to leap after 7 seconds, turn to **311**.

If you wish the Battledroid to leap after 8 seconds, turn to **106**.

8

The tunnel heads north for one kilometre before joining a 400-metre wide crystal tubeway. You continue north towards a distant light at the end of the tubeway, which grows larger and larger until you emerge to see a breathtaking sight.

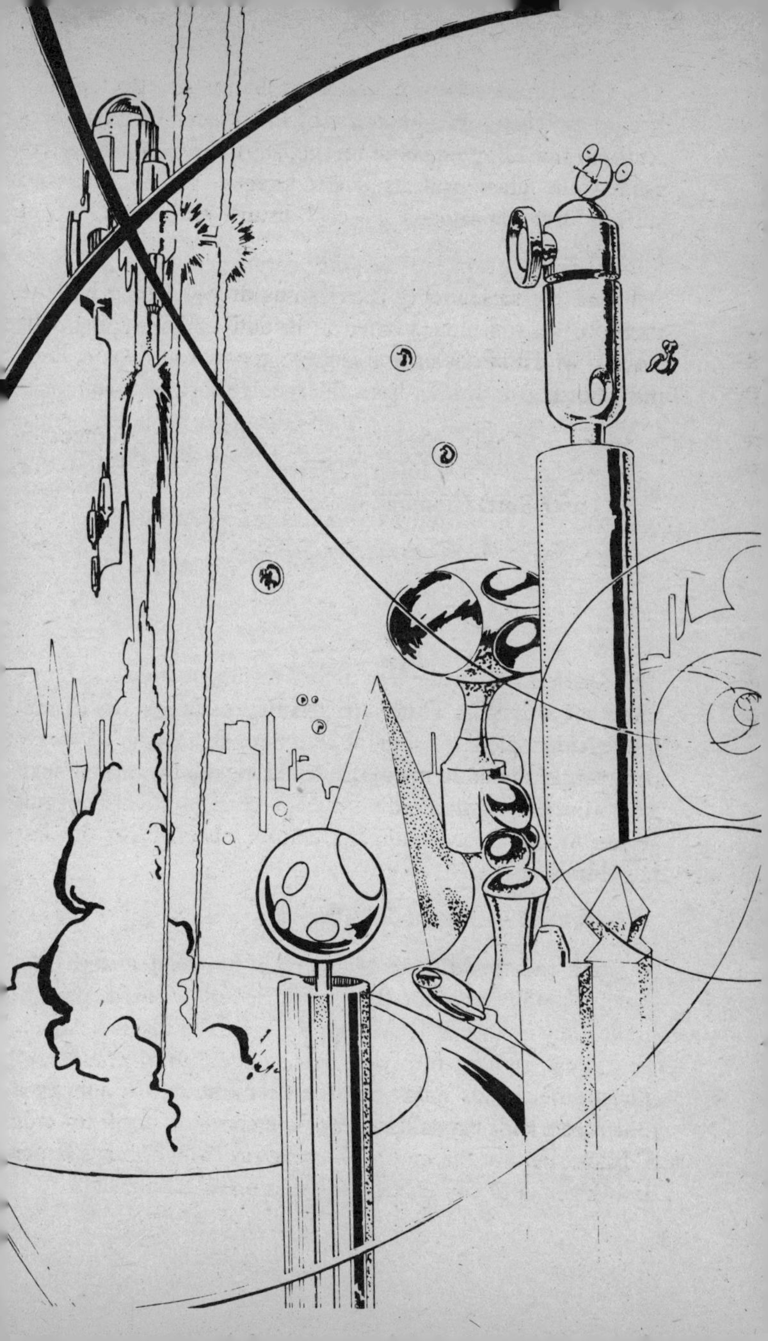

The great glass tubeway stretches out into a vast, underground city, beneath a blue canopy illuminated by a dazzling artificial sun. The entire subterranean metropolis is carved from white Tuskquartz, and is populated by thousands of bustling droids.

The tubeway sweeps between the soaring peaks of kilometre-high towers, and over great, transparent globes that float about the sky furiously driven by their robotic pilots. A lumbering Space Coaster emerges from a spouting spring, and hauls a cargo of Tuskquartz crystals above you, its tracks locked into two shimmering laser-rails. Tiny probes flit constantly against the tubeway wall and study the Battledroid, before dissolving into radiant spirals as they shoot away at light-speed. The Droid Master has not been idle. Turn to **234**.

9

The Lava Beast lies dead at the Battledroid's feet, its Flame Drake rider lifeless on its back. Flames flicker over the causeway as the molten lava thrown up by the furious combat cools. Turn to **218**.

10

You pass your hand over the Intercom bio-reader, and a 3-dimensional image of the Rockworm Security Guard appears on the viewing disc in your control turret. Wiping a trickle of dewy sweat from his furrowed grey brow, he angrily demands in a hoarse croak: "Produce Security Clearance Number or Travel Crystal, or turn back immediately!"

If you have a Travel Crystal and wish to insert it in your control turret facility-receiver, turn to **277**.

If you wish to politely request that the Rockworm lowers the force-gate, turn to **59**.

If you wish to offer your Molecular Disruptor as a bribe, in exchange for the Rockworm lowering the force-gate, turn to **216**.

If you wish to attack the Rockworm, turn to **184**.

11

The tubeway travels up for 200 metres before levelling out and heading south. After 400 metres it comes to a protoplastic air-lock, through which you can see a huge chamber, bathed in a dull blue light. Bubbles of gas seem to float slowly up to disappear in the compartment's roof.

If you wish to use Hover mode to thrust the Battledroid through the air-lock, turn to **296**.

If you wish to use Tracks or Stride mode to propel the Battledroid into the chamber, turn to **120**.

If you wish to travel back down to the main tubeway, turn to **68**.

12

You recover consciousness to see the revolting sight of a bloated Blood Raven lying in front of you. It has gorged itself on your blood. Snatching up your Molecular Disruptor, you fire a shot and blast the creature to oblivion. Roll one dice to assess the damage it has inflicted, and deduct the score from your Life Force.

Miraculously, the Battledroid stands upright at the centre of a broad roadway, and grasping the controls you resume your quest. Turn to **110**.

13

As you enter the dazzling compartment, the Battledroid is engulfed by the brilliant beams of light and seems to break up into millions of tiny, glittering fragments. Then there is blackness.

Gradually a new image begins to form on your viewing screen. The Battledroid has been cast to a new location in the galaxy by a powerful Matter Transporter. Roll one dice.

If the score is 1–3, turn to **237**.

If the score is 4–6, turn to **70**.

14

For two more days the Dragon-Class Space Trucker skims through Caluphex, veering along the Alpha-1 ley-line towards the Caluphex Reaches. During bouts of sub-light travel, you see the emptiness of a galaxy which seems to cower under the threat of Maldraggon's approach. Once, your computer intercepts a crackling Fentusian transmission, translating only the words "*serazith*", meaning "go", and "*gazith*", meaning "*stop*", before your flight fades into silence once more.

Shade in two days on your Status Chart, and turn to **96**.

15

The old man looks down at the crystal, giggles uncontrollably for several seconds, then tuts contemptuously and guides the great metal hand into the corner of the laboratory to sulk. He begins spinning six crystal orbs between the fingers of one hand, and flys a magnificent miniature droid about his head by waving the index finger of the other.

Just as you are wondering what you should do, the silence is shattered by an explosion behind you. Wheeling the Battledroid's turret around, you see a massive black Fentusian Spider Droid emerge through the southern tubeway into the laboratory. Its laser ports slide slowly down as it swoops towards you. The Spider Droid attacks from the rear. Turn to **134**.

16

You emerge in a cavernous chamber, its walls lined with glass, through which shoot intermittent bolts of blue electricity. As the Battledroid lands in the chamber, its gyro-sensors wheezing, your micro-compass spins around to give a reversed reading, as if influenced by some mighty magnetic underground force. (All directions will be given according to your micro-compass).

The chamber is littered with the dusty remains of broken-down droids, ancient dilapidated droid-facilities, and a collection of tangled wires lying on a bed of broken glass.

If you wish to investigate the debris, turn to **104**.

If you wish to ignore the debris, a tunnel descends steeply from the north of the cavern: turn to **253**.

17

The Rockworm Troop form up at various heights around the Battledroid's hull, as you shut down all facilities. Their leader, distinguished by the flowing ermine tail trailing from his laserite oxygen-helm, beckons you onward.

The electric-blue force-gate is lowered, and you guide the Battledroid, surrounded by its triumphant escort, on to the roadway beyond. Turn to **316**.

18

The trail leads to a huge pair of golden gates, shrouded in a flickering blue force-field. Behind them you can see vast skyscrapers, linked with spiralling laser-rails and tubeways, great global buildings hovering in mid-air, and a wide array of buzzing, glowing and flitting unmanned droids, shuttles and communication probes. Only through the gates can you see the sprawling city, for it is surrounded by a concealing force-wall.

You thrust the Battledroid forward, and the gates open quickly as a sombre, disembodied voice declares:

"Your intentions are good. Welcome to the Metropolis of Oric." The Battledroid steps into the city, and the gates close behind you. Turn to **178**.

19

The Battledroid's standard probe-lever picks out the diamond-crystal from its Matter Holder, and thrusts it into the crystal-receiver. The portal shudders and explodes, its debris splintering through the Battledroid's outer shields. Roll two dice and deduct the score from your laser-banks.

If the Battledroid is still functioning, you may proceed along the tubeway, plucking the diamond crystal from the ashes of the portal. Turn to **278**.

20

The Trucker pilot reaches up and programmes the Delta-6 ley-line co-ordinates into the flight-control computer hovering above his right shoulder, mumbling softly, 'Prepare for light-speed engagement.'

The SpaceDrome's Docking-Portals drift slowly apart as the pilot eases himself back in his contoured couch. He thrusts his craft's control column forward heavily, and the Trucker's great engines bellow.

Something seems to be holding the Trucker back, then suddenly the skin on your face tightens. There is a loud bang, and you seem to be flying through a tunnel of swirling colours. The colours merge into a wall of dazzling light, and you are travelling at light-speed through the galaxy. Turn to **274**.

21

The array of black-market weapons and other goods hanging from the belts of eager traders fascinates you, as you push through the bustling crowds. Glancing at the chrono-ring on your finger you are amazed to see that you have been in the SpaceDrome for over half an hour. The Space Trucker should be refuelled and ready to take off by now.

If you wish to hurry back to the Battledroid, turn to **288**.

If you would rather continue investigating the black-markets of Gypsum-2 SpaceDrome, turn to **147**.

22

The flames heat the mercury, causing it to expand, and the glass platform rises slowly to the top of the cavern. The craftsmanship of the lift is perfect, and your silent ascent is completely smooth. You emerge through a portal which slides firmly shut beneath the feet of the Battledroid, hiding the top of the mercury-lift. Looking down at the closed portal through the Battledroid's surveillance cameras, you see that it is now indistinguishable from the rest of a dusty, tunnel floor. Turn to **70**.

23

A cone of white light shoots out from the digi-ring, and the two Fentusians recoil in agony. There is a blinding explosion of light, and the two intruders are evaporated. The digi-ring falls from your finger, its power expended. (Remove it from your Status Chart). Silently thanking the Drome Master for his gift, you attempt to re-activate the Battledroid. It suddenly shudders, bursts into life, and tears itself free from the abandoned Scout-Wasp's claws. Turn to **299**.

24

The Rockworm throws his head back and laughs a hideous cackle, before the radio-communication ends abruptly, and the hologram of the pilot suddenly disappears. The Aero-Limo engages photon-boost and, with a burst of blue flame, disappears into the distance. Turn to **59**.

25

Guiding the Shuttle's grab controls, you wrench the grill away and it clatters loudly to the floor. As you head quickly up the shaft, a menacing shadow descends from above, and a burst of Laser Tracer Rockets flashes past the Shuttle. The noise of your ascent has alerted a gangling Fentusian mutant, its leathery body crudely daubed with black and orange Lizard Camo-pigment. Its three deformed heads are thrown back on their sinewy necks by the thrust of the heavily-armed Space-Scoot to which it clings. Lowering the Shuttle's laser port, you enter battle. (Range = 50m)

MOUNTED FENTUSIAN TRI-MUTANT: Attack = 12 Defence = 7 Absorption = 0 Laser Reserves = 10.

If you defeat the mutant, turn to **257**.

26

The fury of the firestorm throws the Battledroid to its knees. A burning rain lashes your turret, and the enormous fire-rocks begin to pierce your defence-shields. Suddenly, a burning meteor looms from the livid, lightning-torn sky. It plummets towards you, and smashes into the Battledroid.

Roll two dice to assess damage, and roll two dice to determine which area of the Battledroid has been hit. If you have a defence facility in this area, subtract its absorption from the damage. Deduct the damage total from your laser-banks.

If you are still alive, turn to **185**.

27

As you speak the name Gan Tamil-Rath, the turquoise cloak suddenly collapses, revealing a small droid, swaying unsteadily on its one jointed leg. Thousands of wires erupt wildly from its glass turret. Within the turret appears the flickering image of a small man in a green robe, his swollen bald skull embellished with a circular blue tattoo. He shouts to you in a high-pitched voice:

"Gan Tamil-Rath, last of the Droid Masters, lives in the deepest, darkest cave at the very heart of the planet Oric. He is hidden by the great Tuskquartz mines that emerge in the Metropolis north of the Hot Spring Plains. Take this gift, that you may honour the Master of Oric."

The communication ends as a small sculpture of an orb within a blazing circle emerges from the Battledroid's Matter Transporter. The circle revolves continuously about the orb.

Note down the Droid Master's Symbol on your Status Chart and turn to **157**.

28

Water starts to splash into your control turret, and life-support gauges descend rapidly into the red danger zones. You struggle for breath, and frantically seek an exit from the water-filled cavern. Roll one dice:

If you roll 1–5, deduct 1 point from your life-force, and roll again. If your life force falls to zero, you have failed in your mission.

If you roll a 6, you find an exit tunnel, filled with steam at high pressure, descending from the bottom of the lake, directly below the geyser's blow-hole. Turn to **126**.

29

Tilting the Battledroid down on its belly, you guide it slowly forward into the Trucker's cargo-bay. The bay is stripped down to its steel framework, and echoes emptily as the Battledroid settles at its centre. Several tall figures, their faces concealed in dark helmets and their bodies covered with black space armour swathed in grey cloaks, sit high above you in curious transparent pods attached to the cargo-bay's walls.

Your pilot, his face still concealed beneath a black visor, sprints down the cargo-bay's footbridge alongside your droid, his heavy boots ringing against the steel plates, his cloak billowing up behind him. Glancing up at you, he leaps into the air-shuttle which will carry him to the Space Trucker's control tower.

Note down that you are travelling in Space Trucker Gamma and turn to **127**.

30

The Spider Droid swoops past the Battledroid, puzzled by your reluctance to enter combat. The golden-skinned creature meanwhile attaches the final component, and the old man thrusts his levy-disc up into the roof of the laboratory.

You re-activate the Battledroid, to find its machinery silent, its controls sliding smoothly up to mould into your fingers. Add 2 to your initial Attack Capacity, 2 to your initial Defence Capacity, 6 to your Laser Reserves and Laser Reserves Maximum, and 2 to your Pilot Skill.

You thrust the revitalised Battledroid towards the wheeling Spider Droid. Turn to **134**.

31

The Battledroid glides smoothly above the Viper-Coaster as it accelerates through the force-gate. The Rockworm guard, his eyes shot red with anger, beckons furiously at you, but is powerless to stop you as the Coaster's hull shields you from the electric beams. Add 2 to your Pilot Skill and turn to **110**.

32

You press your palm over the Automated Claw's bio-sensor, and the Claw shoots out towards the robotron, its steel-link fingers splayed wildly. The robotron waves its arms in alarm as your facility knocks it clumsily to the ground. The Claw pierces the Tuskquartz Globe's anti-gravity laser-banks, and there is a dazzling explosion, throwing the shrieking robotron violently across the chamber. Roll one die and deduct the score from your laser banks.

If the Battledroid still functions, you thrust it through the tubeway heading north, leaving the robotron in a crumpled heap in the corner murmuring:

"W-w-w-welcome to the Droid Master's chambers... Welcome to the Droid Master's chambers..." Turn to **8**.

33

Setting the Battledroid to auto-pilot, you touch the Shuttle's bio-reader and your pilot-couch descends gently through the floor of the control turret. There is a low hiss as the air-lift carries you down through the Battledroid, and positions you behind the Shuttle's controls. Rolling the palm of your hand over the control sphere, you guide the Shuttle away from its socket and up through the eerie mist to the Battledroid's control turret.

Guiding the Shuttle to the lowest Limpet, you attempt to dislodge it with your craft's grab. It is firmly attached, though, and its chant of death grows louder as the grab makes contact.

Two buttons protrude from the Limpet Droid. One is green and labelled with the letter "G"; the other is red and marked "S".

If you wish to use the Shuttle's claw to press the green "G" button, turn to 117.

If you wish to use the Shuttle's claw to press the red "S" button, turn to 149.

34

Deduct 2 from your laser-banks. You head north according to your micro-compass bearings, until eventually the crimson sea ends and the grey lava causeway rises on to a large plateau. Steaming springs burble all across the plateau, and geysers gush 250-metre waterspouts at regular intervals.

The Battledroid's sensors suddenly indicate a creature heading towards you across the lava plateau at high speed. Engaging the Image Enhancer, you see a small grey creature slithering rapidly across the lava-bed. It resembles a giant slug, and leaves a silver trail of slime behind it.

The Lava Louse suddenly springs from the plateau and hurls itself up against the Battledroid's viewing screen, seeming to grow as it passes through your defence shields. The Battledroid has no data on this creature, and you must carefully select an attack facility without guidance from the computer.

Choose one of your attack facilities, and turn to **236**.

35

The Drome Master powers his craft into an air-lock in the Battledroid's chest and emerges seconds later in your control turret, still tumbling along in the Drome-Walker. Clasping the throat of his black silk robes with one hand, he points the long thin fingers of the other at you and asks in a high-pitched squeak:

"What business have you and your clumsy droid in my SpaceDrome, hmm?"

If you have a Travel Crystal and wish to give it to the Drome Master, demanding immediate passage on a Space Trucker, turn to **229**.

If you wish to explain that you believe your Battledroid can defeat the evil Fentusian Maldraggon, turn to **93**.

36

The two-headed silhouette of the mercenary suddenly fills the control tower's entrance portal. There is a loud bang, and you feel something whistle past your ear as the turret fills with black smoke.

As the smoke slowly clears, you see the two Fentusians lying dead at the mercenary's feet, their bodies peppered with tiny holes. The mercenary stands proudly nodding his heads, an antique blunderbuss cradled in his arms, its gaping snout still billowing smoke. Thanking him humbly for saving your life, you re-activate the Battledroid. Despite the millions of holes that now riddle the inside of your turret, the Battledroid shudders back to life, tearing itself from the claws of the abandoned Scout-Wasp. Turn to **299**.

37

As you thrust the Battledroid forward on to the light-bridge, a large platinum portal, from which hangs a heavily-armoured Rockworm, swings shut behind you. The Rockworm Police swarm forward 200 metres below you, and the light-bridge begins to slowly retract into the Security Bay. Your only hope of escape is to thrust the Battledroid along the light-bridge into the Space Hangar before it recedes completely. Turn to **235**.

38

The Battledroid shudders as it shakes off the residue of the pink liquid, blasting it from your viewing screen with its hydrowipers. After running a random systems' check, you propel the Battledroid onwards.

The tubeway soon turns and begins to descend, and you plummet further and further into Oric's core. The tubeway's glass walls steam up with the heat of the planet's heart, but are cleared by a ring of light which runs rapidly along the tubeway every few seconds. A tiny maintenance droid also hurrys past you, its suckered feet pattering against the glass walls as it darts rapidly about, searching for faults.

After some ten kilometres, the tubeway emerges in a massive underground chamber. Turn to **228**.

39

The Battledroid's probe-lever selects the gold crystal from its Matter Holder, and extends it into the crystal-receiver. The crystal-receiver instantly spits out the crystal and the portal explodes. Roll two dice and deduct the score from your laser-banks.

If the Battledroid is still functioning, you retrieve the gold crystal and proceed through the wreckage of the portal. Turn to **298**.

40

Your stomach churns sickeningly as you look down on the bodies of the Rockworms scattered beneath the Battledroid. The force-gate ahead of you is now unmanned and lowered. Swallowing hard, you thrust the Battledroid on to the roadway beyond. Turn to **110**.

41

You manage to engage photon-boost in Hover mode, thrusting the Battledroid back up towards the mercury-lift. The Crevasse Crawler loses its hold and its snaking body plummets down to the cavern floor. Roll one dice and deduct the score from your straining laser-banks.

If the Battledroid still functions, you urge it back up to the silver disc at the centre of the causeway. Turn to **150**.

42

The Battledroid slips from your control and Oric's glowing surface rises rapidly up to meet you. You hit the ground with a sickening thump, the Battledroid's gyro-sensors belching out great jets of steam as they cushion your control turret against the impact. Roll one dice and deduct the score from your laser-banks.

The impact has sunk the Battledroid up to its waist in the middle of a huge causeway of solidified lava. The causeway runs through the middle of a lake of molten lava, its crimson surface bubbling and boiling. Engaging photon-boost, you thrust the Battledroid out of its crater and land on the roadway.

If your Time-Chart shows seven or more days, turn to 92.

If your Time-Chart shows six or less days, turn to 299.

43

After following the roadway around to the right, the hulking Securi-Pod suddenly veers off the road. A circular silver portal in the cliff-face slides open, and the heavy grey craft descends into a dark tunnel.

If you have Satellite-Informed Radar Scan, you may guide the Battledroid headfirst into the tunnel by engaging Hover mode: turn to 294.

Alternatively, you may follow the roadway as it turns north and approaches the towering blue wall of an electric force-gate: turn to 122.

44

Grasping the controls of the probe-lever, you select the silver crystal from the Battledroid's Matter Holder, and press it into the crystal-receiver. The portal slides silently open. Retrieving the crystal, you continue down the tubeway. Turn to 315.

45

The Fentusian Gulf's mists suddenly change, merging into a heavy, ragged grey veil which clings to the Battledroid's hull.

You engage extra thrust to penetrate it, and as your control turret pushes through, you are greeted by a sight which makes your heart sink. A Fentusian Battle Fleet of some fifty sleek black Space Cruisers drifts lazily through the gulf, in the clear dock created by the ragged grey radar screen. As you heave back on the Battledroid's controls, a huge Eagle-Class Fighter sweeps up behind you. For the first two rounds, it attacks from the rear. (Range = 1km)

FENTUSIAN EAGLE-FIGHTER: Attack = 16 Defence = 8 Absorption = 2 Laser Reserves = 20 (Gain Bonus for Rotary Laser-Bomb Launcher) (Immune to Negative-Ion Flame-Thrower)

If you defeat the Eagle-Fighter, turn to **167**.

46

The Droid Master's Gladiator Security Automaton dangles from its umbilical control-pipe, its massive feet carving a groove in the steel floor as it swings to and fro. You exit through a great glass tubeway, heading north, the throb of the Battledroid's laser-banks echoing through the tunnel. Turn to **259**.

47

Even from the great height of the Battledroid's turret, you feel dwarfed by the imposing structures of the SpaceDrome. Immense silver globes joined by spiralling steel tubeways protrude from sheer walls of thick glass which ascend into the sky to curve into a massive steel-ribbed dome.

The Hover-Bugs which swarm about the immense doors of the entrance portal scatter as you propel the Battledroid into the building. Turn to **130**.

48

You travel along the causeway for three kilometres before it comes to a junction. Molten lava laps gently over the side of the causeway, spitting scorching bubbles at the Battledroid's feet.

If you have fought a Lava Beast and its Flame Drake rider during your quest, turn to **218**.

If you have not, turn to **246**.

49

Your computer searches through data-banks for an appropriate response, and overrides your Gamma-Wave Intercom.

If your computer capacity is 10 or more, turn to **310**.

If your computer capacity is 9 or less, turn to **121**.

50

The laser-dock seems to hold the Battledroid fast, but switching to Hover and engaging maximum photon-boost, you feel it begin to ease its grip. You have no choice but to engage full emergency power, and thrust a massive amount of energy through the Battledroid's Hover Jets. As you do so there is a tremendous roar, your control-turret vibrates violently, and then the Battledroid wrenches itself free and soars rapidly up towards the ceiling. Roll two dice, and deduct the total from your laser-banks.

Three huge tubeways run along the ceiling of the Holding Bay and join up in a great glass globe at its centre. A sliding portal allows you to thrust the Battledroid up into this junction, and you can now follow a tubeway north, south or west, into the SpaceDrome.

If you wish to go west, turn to **142**.

If you wish to go south, turn to **214**.

If you wish to go north, turn to **252**.

51

You guide the Battledroid through the gaping mouth of the cargo-bay, and land it gently on a steel floor. Several grey-cloaked figures perch high above you in transparent capsules attached to the bay's walls.

As you thrust the Battledroid's turret forward into the Droid-Link, the control tower of the Trucker appears before you. The pilot wears a heavy grey cloak over black steel space armour, his face obscured by the dark visor of a space helm. Turn to **145**.

52

The Battledroid's Flight-Computer co-ordinates begin to spin randomly, and you swoop uncontrollably over Oric's surface, losing all bearings. The Battledroid's laser-banks throb and its engines howl, as you search desperately for a place to land among the burning pools of lava that cover Oric. Roll one dice:

If you score 1 or 2, turn to **42**.

If you score 3 or 4, turn to **317**.

If you score 5 or 6, turn to **199**.

53

You follow the Tuskquartz Denizen down a short tubeway before it scampers off into one of a network of tiny, rough tunnels, presumably mined by its own shovel-boned claws.

The tunnels are too small even for an Independent Information Probe to travel, and you continue down the white marble tubeway.

It emerges in a vast hexagonal chamber, formed from enormous sheets of tinted plexoglass, through which you can make out the misted figures of Tuskquartz Denizens scrabbling through their labyrinthine lairs.

The floor of the chamber is a great pool of pink neon liquid from which protrudes a long sinuous black tube, terminating in a small, spherical droid, heavily armed with photon-phasers. It is positioned to defend a huge, glass tubeway which spirals elegantly out of the far side of the chamber. The droid's phaser ports swivel stiffly towards you.

If you have Sonic Punch and wish to activate it, turn to 215.

If you wish to plunge the Battledroid into the pink liquid, turn to 156.

54

Suddenly a Mutant-Spore plummets through the red-tinged vapour above you. The sickly green body of a Flesh Mutant fills this huge orb, its wet eyes pressed hideously against the glass. Maldraggon has cast these foul creations throughout the galaxies, and this one seems to have sniffed out the Battledroid. Your Rockworm guards urge you to flee north with them to the SpaceDrome.

If you wish to flee with your Rockworm escort, turn to 172.

If you wish to ignore their orders and attack the Mutant-Spore, turn to 224.

55

As you finish recharging, a small droid suddenly darts out from one of two tubeways in the northern wall of the gallery.

A tiny, glowing thread trails from its hull back into the tunnel. The droid shoots up to the Battledroid and spits a laser beam into your hull, before the glowing thread seems to tug it back into the tubeway. Deduct 1 from your laser-banks. Your computer's enemy-monitor identifies the attacking automaton as an 'Angler Droid'.

If you wish to pursue the Angler Droid into the tubeway, turn to **226**.

If you wish to exit north through the second tubeway, turn to **112**.

56

The fantastic crimson surface of Oric rises up out of the mists before you. Laser-rail causeways stretch from its glowing surface to the distant marbled face of Zzyus which looms ominously in the distance. Oric's atmosphere is alive with the flitting of unmanned probes and shuttles, in stark contrast to the paralysed galaxy you have left behind.

Your viewing screen suddenly becomes animated with the laser-tracery of a computer-coded message.

"Encoded Distress Call:
Source Code: Vizo Rath, Holy Emperor of Anthracitex-9, Overseer of Caluphex. Message: On mercy mission to Oric. Betrayed by Maldraggon. I am besieged. Please assist. End."

It seems that your enemy is close at hand.

If you have Gamma-Wave Intercom and wish to contact Vizo Rath, turn to **179**.

If you do not, turn to **286**.

57

As you pass your hand over its bio-reader, the Mutant Sensory Unit activates, and begins swaying from screen to screen, above the jerking heads of their robotic operators. You verbally order the Battledroid's computer to accept all information directly: add 3 to your computer capacity.

Glancing down from your towering control turret, you see the Rockworm troops stirring from their slumber in the Securi-Pod. Engaging photon-boost, you thrust the Battledroid across the room and through a circular portal. Turn to **130**.

58

The Battledroid's probe-lever selects the silver crystal from its Matter Holder, and prods it into the crystal-receiver. The portal swings open, then slams shut, with a massive explosion. Roll two dice and deduct the total from your laser-banks.

If the Battledroid is still functioning, you retrieve the silver crystal from the debris of the portal and continue along the tubeway. Turn to **298**.

59

Suddenly, as the Intercom image disappears, a large silver portal in the centre of the roadway slides open and a troop of Inter-Galactic Police, ten hulking Rockworms armed with stun-rods, emerge from the tunnel below. Mounted on Anti-Gravity Sleds, they make a rush for your control turret.

*If you wish to combat the Rockworm Troop, turn to **188**.*

*If you would prefer to shut down the Battledroid and surrender, turn to **17**.*

60

The Lava Beast fights desperately to defend its young, showering the Battledroid with molten lava as it lunges at your control tower. Deduct 2 from your attack capacity for the duration of this combat if you are in Tracks mode of movement. (Range = 100m)

LAVA BEAST AND FLAME DRAKE: Attack = 15 Defence = 5 Absorption = 3 Laser Reserves = 16. (Gain Bonus for Laser Port, Psi-Exuder) (Immune to Negative-Ion Flame Thrower)

*If you win and wish to flee north, turn to **70**.*

*If you win and wish to flee south, turn to **189**.*

61

The mercenary urges his smoking craft alongside and docks with one of the Battledroid's attack or work facility sockets. He uses his engines to hover and make his craft, in effect, weightless. Note that you have the mercenary-shuttle on your Status Chart.

You pass your palm over the Battledroid's "co-pilot" bio-reader, a facility you often fooled with when the Battledroid was at the museum. A hologram of the mercenary instantly appears alongside you, placing him in full communication, as if he really were seated beside your pilot couch. Add 1 to your attack capacity, and turn to **163**.

62

As the Black Widow Spider Droid swoops menacingly towards you, your Image Enhancer relays the grotesque features of the evil Fentusian Overlord Maldraggon and his Death-General, Violwart, behind the droid's controls. Their craft bristles with photon-phasers, laser-ports and disruptor cannon, and it is shrouded in the azure mist of a powerful

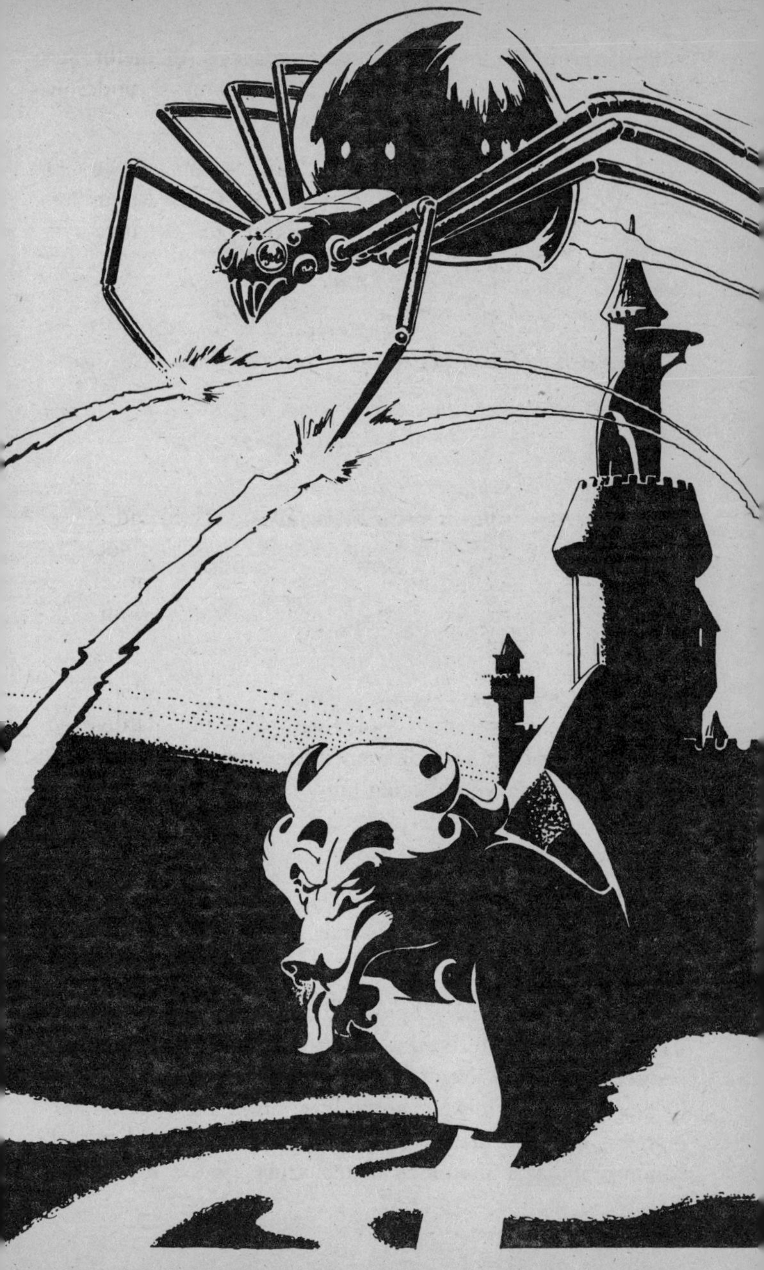

defensive force-field. It will undoubtedly provide the greatest test yet for your aged Battledroid. Gan Tamil-Rath's Soul-Server mans a laser-pod as you enter combat.

If you have a Mind-Choker and wish to contact your Craft Master, turn to 220.

If you have a 'z' beside your computer capacity, add 2 to your attack capacity for the duration of this battle.

If you have a mercenary-shuttle noted on your Status Chart, add 2 to your attack capacity for the duration of this battle.

If your computer capacity equals 15 or more, add 2 to your defence capacity for the duration of this combat.

If your pilot skill equals 12 or more, add 2 to your defence capacity for the duration of this combat. (Range = 2km)

FENTUSIAN BLACK WIDOW SPIDER DROID: Attack = 20 Defence = 9 Absorption = 4 Laser Reserves = 30 (Gain Bonus for Laser Port).

If you defeat the Spider Droid and have Vizo Rath in your control turret, turn to 320.

If you defeat the Spider Droid but do not have Vizo Rath with you, turn to 4.

63

The viewing-column immediately bursts into life, depicting the ley-line Space Trucker routes available from Anthracitex-9 to Oric in the Fentusian Gulf.

The quickest route is brightly illuminated. You must plot a course along the Delta-6 ley-line to the planet Ironis-2, in the Caluphix Reaches. Then you follow the Alpha-2 ley-line as it weaves between the twin stars of Platinus and orbits the planets Jethal and Zol, before plunging into the Fentusian

Gulf. A small read-out below the map of your galaxy reads: "Oric: a volcanic planet orbiting Zzyus in the Fentusian Gulf. Features: Oric is beyond normal Trucker routes. It is so small that it often registers on radar as a large, slow-moving space craft."

You recall the Probe and continue north along the tubeway. Add 2 to your computer capacity and turn to **252**.

64

The cooled-lava causeway branches out in three different directions.

If you wish to go south according to your micro-compass, turn to **18**.

If you wish to go south-east according to your micro-compass, turn to **98**.

If you wish to go south-west according to your micro-compass, turn to **162**.

65

The ferocious combat cripples the Pirate Trucker, and you thrust the Battledroid quickly away from it. The hulking craft spirals down towards Zol and explodes as it penetrates the planet's atmosphere. You select Space movement and thrust the Battledroid along the Alpha-2 ley-line, descending into the mists of the Fentusian Gulf. Turn to **279**.

66

Leaving the Laser Recharger behind you, you head south according to your micro-compass readings. Staring up in awe at the sweeping fluorescent laser-rails, sheer glass towers and floating glass probe-docks, you urge the fully-charged Battledroid onward. Turn to **318**.

67

You head north with the high-pitched scream of the SpaceDrome's emergency-alert siren echoing along the gaping black tubeway, until you reach a crossroads. A visual display unit informs you that the north tubeway leads to the Security Bay, the east tubeway to the Vapour Monitor, and the west tubeway to the Droid Library. The west tubeway is large enough only for the Manually-Operated Shuttle.

You must eventually find your way to the Docking Hangar. Firstly, though, you would like to find your Craft Master, who is currently studying at the SpaceDrome. You would also like to find out information about the planet Oric and the Fentusian Gulf.

If you go north, turn to **142**.

If you go east, turn to **214**.

If you have the Manually-Operated Shuttle, and wish to head west, turn to **232**.

68

The Battledroid steps into a beautifully-mined white marble tubeway. Some sort of large rune is painted in red on the floor before you, and intermittent pulses of blue light race along the tubeway's walls. Several metres in front of you, a smaller tubeway ascends from the roof of the tunnel.

If you were bitten by a lava-louse earlier in your adventure and have felt no ill effects, turn to **247**.

If you wish to head south along the main tubeway, turn to **255**.

If you wish to propel the Battledroid up into the smaller tunnel, turn to **11**.

69

You thrust the Battledroid down towards the north-east Hot Spring Plains of Oric, entering an atmosphere choked with heavy, white Tuskquartz dust. Hydro-wipers blast the dust from your viewing screen but it quickly clogs your exhaust valves, making the Battledroid's great engines moan in protest. Your craft kicks and shudders violently as you battle with its controls, regretting ruefully the days of your apprenticeship spent hiding in the head of an old Aqua-Robotron to avoid your lessons on the Flight Simulator.

Roll one dice and add the score to your pilot skill. Add 2 if you have Satellite-Informed Radar Scan.

*If the score is 11 or more, turn to **199**.*

*If the score is 10 or less, turn to **52**.*

70

You emerge in a gaping horizontal tunnel, its beautifully crafted walls illuminated by a silver lichen.

*If you wish to head north, where the tunnel starts to climb, turn to **203**.*

*If you wish to travel south along the passageway, turn to **309**.*

71

As you finally emerge from the crowds, you are horrified to see your Space Trucker's engines blasting out jets of fire. The white paint daubed on the side of the Trucker has peeled off to reveal the golden hawk emblem of a Space Pirate.

Shielding your face from the heat of the Trucker's engines, you sprint the length of the docking-bay and, clambering up the side of the ship, look into the control tower. The pirate has removed his helmet, revealing the distinctive transparent skin of a Fentusian, which allows you to see the green blood throbbing through his brain and pulsing veins. He turns, grins cruelly at you, and thrusts his Trucker's control column forward. You are thrown clear as the Trucker, and your Battledroid, disappear into the galaxy. Your mission ends here.

72

The pink anti-gravity gas has made the Battledroid weightless, but the power of your attack facilities thrusts you back down to the floor of the chamber. Switching on the Battledroid's Audio Transmitters, you ask the old man, who reclines far below you, for his help against Maldraggon.

The old man conjures and weaves with his fingers, and a small glass orb rises from the laboratory floor and breathes a thin white mist about him, as he speaks in a low, calming voice:

"I am a Time-Weaver, Master of Droids. You must prove your worthiness to seek my assistance. To this end I will set you a simple riddle:

> You carry three crystals, all that I own,
> Give that to me with the weight of one stone.'

He snuggles into the great hand that carries him, and sinks his head into the collar of his voluminous cloak.

You have no idea how much each crystal weighs, or indeed how heavy was the ancient imperial measurement of one stone. Which crystal do you eject through the Battledroid's Matter Transporter?

If you select the diamond crystal, turn to **262**.

If you select the gold crystal, turn to **313**.

If you select the silver crystal, turn to **15**.

73

You surprise the Fentusian Space Fighter: begin combat from stage 10. (Range = 1km)

> FENTUSIAN SPACE FIGHTER: Attack = 14 Defence = 6 Absorption = 3 Laser Reserves = 10 (Gain Bonus for Rotary Laser-Bomb Launcher) (Immune to Negative-Ion Flame-Thrower)

If you defeat the Space Fighter, turn to **94**.

74

The Aero-Limo swoops beneath the Battledroid's huge legs and accelerates back up the granite roadway. You continue to follow the pathway as it turns northwards and approaches an electric force-gate manned by a member of the Rockworm Inter-Galactic Police. Turn to **81**.

75

You activate the Sonic Punch, aligning its computer-guidance controls with the mercury-platform. The Sonic Punch shoots down and smashes into the silver disc, with a deafening explosion. The mercury-lift sinks momentarily, before rising back up to its original level. The Battledroid's 'eagle-owl audio-sensors' detect a scrabbling, scratching sound far below you as some creature stirs, woken by the Sonic Punch.

Suddenly, a massive, grey, snake-like creature emerges over the side of the causeway and strikes out at the Battledroid with its barbed teeth.

> The Crevasse Crawler attacks from behind. (Range = 0)

CREVASSE CRAWLER: Attack = 12 Defence = 7 Absorption = 1 Life Reserves = 25 (Gain Bonus for Psi-Exuder) (Immune to Sonic Punch)

If the Crevasse Crawler rolls an 11 or 12 on its attack dice, turn to **243**.

If you defeat the Crevasse Crawler, turn to **150**.

76

As the tubeway twists and turns, the Battledroid's Wind-sensors indicate a strong breeze gusting down from the north. 400 metres along the tubeway, a small square shaft heads off to the east, large enough only for the Independent Information Probe.

If you have the Probe facility and wish to depatch it along the shaft, turn to **133**.

If you do not have this facility, or do not wish to use it, you must continue north. Turn to **252**.

77

You come to a platform made from grey columns of cooled lava. Three lava-causeways head out from the platform, jutting across the bubbling sea. According to the Battledroid's micro-compass, the causeways head north-east, east, and south.

If you wish to head north-east, according to your micro-compass, turn to **275**.

If you wish to head east according to your micro-compass, turn to **208**.

If you wish to head south according to your micro-compass, turn to **162**.

If you have Satellite-Informed Radar Scan and wish to scan this area of Oric, turn to **295**.

78

After travelling only a few metres down the shaft, the Battledroid suddenly flinches and retracts its legs. Something is stimulating its Human-Reaction Sensors. The computer confirms your fears of danger, announcing:

"Water Mutant – Range: 2 metres – Highly dangerous."

From the control turret, you cannot see the monster that attacks you from below.

If you wish to engage photon-boost and escape up the tunnel, deduct 3 from your laser-banks and turn to **253**.

If you wish to move into combat mode, turn to **210**.

79

You slide the tokens into the Battledroid's Matter Transporter, and they instantly emerge in front of the Trucker pilot. He turns and smiles, whispering: "Space Pirates are fast, but Smugglers are faster, Battledroid pilot." He engages photon-boost and you soar into the mists of the Fentusian Gulf, the other Space Trucker disappearing into the distance. Turn to 319.

80

You grasp the controls of the Battledroid's probe-lever and, using the vidi-screens, pluck the gold crystal from the Battledroid's Matter Holder. You guide the lever forward, and insert the crystal in its receiver. There is a dull click, and the portal swings slowly open.

Pausing only to retrieve the crystal, you continue along the tubeway. Turn to 278.

81

Deduct 2 from your laser-banks if travelling by Hover. This force-gate's guard is a deformed Rockworm, the knuckles of his grey-scaled claws resting heavily on the dusty roadway between his feet. A large silver ring, emerging from the matted hair of his flaring nostrils, is joined with a link-chain to his polished black breast-plate. His hulking frame, silhouetted against the dazzling blue force-field behind him, looks tiny as you stare down from the dizzy height of the Battledroid's control tower.

The five-metre tall Rockworm looks up in astonishment as you approach. His great bloodshot eyes stare cruelly towards you as he draws his stun-rod from a dull-black leather belt and presses his wrist-communicator up against his scaly mouth.

If you have a Travel Crystal and wish to insert it in your control turret facility-receiver, turn to **277**.

If you wish to thrust the Battledroid into the electric force-gate, turn to **209**.

If you have a Gamma-Wave Intercom and wish to communicate with the Rockworm, turn to **10**.

If you wish to attack the Rockworm, turn to **184**.

82

You de-activate the computer's master switch, but the computer continues to function. An image of the Flame Drake's mournful face appears on the viewing screen, and the computer whispers, in a voice ghoulishly imitating your own speech-pattern: "You no longer control me, Battledroid pilot, I have a new master now."

Furiously, you begin wrenching wires from the computer console. Roll one dice:

If the score is 3 or less, deduct the score from your computer capacity and roll again. If your computer capacity reaches zero, the Battledroid's brains have been devoured by this robotic parasite, and your mission is over.

If the score is 4 or more, the computer de-activates with a dull moan of protest, and the manual controls and monitor screens for all your attack facilities rise up from your console. The Flame Drake, seeing your attack facilities active again, detaches the Techno-Leach, and flees across the Metropolis. Turn to **318**.

83

A large bead of sweat breaks from the pilot's frowning forehead and his face reddens as he smiles awkwardly at you, his crumpled cigar falling to the floor. Grasping the Trucker's control-column with trembling hands, he whispers: "Why, of course I'd be honoured to carry you into the gulf . . . free of charge . . . sir." He nervously engages photon-boost, and the Trucker swoops into the wispy cloud of the Fentusian Gulf. Turn to **219**.

84

The Shuttle glides out of the shadows into the centre of the chamber, as Death-General Violwart, with a deep-throated chuckle disappears into the Black Widow Spider Droid. The droid's belly hangs open for a few seconds, and as you dart towards it, the Shuttle's sensory probes relay the Spider Droid's technical data back to the Battledroid. Place a 'z' beside your computer capacity.

As the Spider Droid prepares to take off, you realize that you will need the firepower of the Battledroid to stop it. Powering the Shuttle's engines to full thrust, you smash through the spire's glass roof and sweep around the Wolf Tower, back to the Battledroid. Turn to **303**.

85

On the Trucker's screen you see the dark shadows of Space disturbed by a small planet, its swirling turquoise and azure surface circled by three black satellites. Your computer identifies it as Ironis-2, and indicates a live radio signal emanating from a colony on its south face.

If you have a Gamma-Wave Intercom and wish to contact the Ironis-2 colony, turn to **281**.

If you do not have this facility, or would prefer to leave Ironis-2 undisturbed, turn to **157**.

86

After climbing for about 60 metres, the tunnel suddenly descends again, so steeply that you have to briefly engage Hover mode. It slowly levels out, and the rough-hewn walls become smoothly chiselled, as the passageway heads south for two kilometres. Turn to **264**.

87

As the Battledroid ascends into the thick scarlet cloud, a choking red mist billows into the control turret, blistering and burning your face and hands. Through the heavily clouded sky hurtle thousands of Blood Ravens. These ruthless predators, their blood-red eyes gazing hideously at you, soar madly into the Battledroid's hull. Some are thrown back by your defence shields, and others scrabble and scratch at the Battledroid's armour, searching for a way into your turret. You must fight off their attack. (Range = 0)

BLOOD RAVENS: Attack = 9 Defence = 9 Life Reserves = 15 (Gain bonus for Psi-Exuder) (Immune to Sonic Punch)

If you have not finished the combat after 3 rounds, turn to **260**.

If you defeat the Blood Ravens, turn to **175**.

88

To your horror, a huge Fentusian Scout-Wasp swoops down through the mist, clawing at your control tower with massive steel talons, and launching attacks from two eye-like laser ports. A crystal turret bobs above its hull on the end of a jointed tower, and it is steadied by the beating of four huge, leathery wings.

Thin, luminous yellow wires trail from the Scout Wasp, miles into the distance, so giving it a false radar-reading.

As you move into combat, the crimson surface of Oric appears through the mist beyond the Scout-Wasp. (Range = 2km)

FENTUSIAN SCOUT WASP: Attack = 14 Defence = 7 Absorption = 2 Laser Reserves = 13 (Gain Bonus for Laser Port) (Immune to Negative-Ion Flame Thrower)

If the Scout-Wasp inflicts 6 or more points of actual damage in one round, do not deduct the damage, but turn to 302.

If you defeat the Scout-Wasp, turn to 56.

89

You activate the Mutant Sensory Unit, and the mutant weaves its head slowly out of the facility socket. Sniffing the ground, it suddenly recoils in fear and horror, before retracting back into the Battledroid. Your computer reads:

"Mutant Sensory Unit detects scent of a fully grown Sewer Beast. Would advise Battledroid pilot to proceed on Tracks to avoid disturbance of loose flag-stones containing this creature." Turn to 266.

90

All exits from the chamber are sealed shut by the darting craft of the Drome Master. You are hopelessly trapped, as the Rockworm troops swarm about the Battledroid's tracks. Admitting defeat, you deactivate the Battledroid and begin your slow descent from the control tower, to surrender. You have failed your mission before even leaving Anthracitex-9.

91

You thrust the Battledroid down through the blackened remains of the Water Mutant, and continue down the shaft. Switching to turret-camera you see, to your horror, that the mutant is slowly regenerating, translucent white flesh quivering out from beneath its charred, black husk. Engaging extra boost, you flee from the indestructible mutation.

The Battledroid's hover jets roar as you descend for over a kilometre, before the mine-shaft joins a brightly lit, gaping glass tubeway, heading north. Selecting a movement mode, you thrust the Battledroid along it. Turn to **183**.

92

In the distance you can hear a menacing, high-pitched whine. It grows louder, and suddenly a spinning, wheeling, automated gun-ship whistles overhead, its laser ports spitting death. Three laser bolts soar through your outer defence shields. Roll one dice to assess damage, and two dice to see where the Battledroid has been hit. If you have a defence facility in the area hit, deduct its absorption from the damage. Deduct any remaining damage from your laser banks.

The automated gun-ship has already become a small speck on the horizon, in the direction indentified by the Battledroid's micro-compass as north.

If you wish to engage the automated gun-ship in combat, turn to **251**.

If you do not, turn to **299**.

93

The Drome Master's expression of astonishment slowly turns to a smile. Scratching his bald head with a disjointed finger, he squeals, "I am breaking all regulations, but I feel that I must help you. Follow the northern tubeway and find your way to the Docking Hangar. I will order you a Space Trucker."

As he tumbles out of the control turret, the Drome Master

fires a golden bubble which floats up and rests against your viewing screen. (Note this down on your Status Chart.) As the Drome-Walker emerges into the Entrance Bay and shoots out through a small portal, you guide the Battledroid north into a wide tubeway. Turn to **67**.

94

The Battledroid swoops down towards Oric's glowing surface. The tiny planet's atmosphere is choked with the dust kicked up by generations of Tuskquartz miners. It clogs your viewing screen and viewing cameras as fast as their hydro-wipers can clean them. Your vision obscured, you soar into two glowing laser-rails, and the Battledroid reels from your control. Rueing the days you spent fooling among the museum exhibits, playing truant from your lessons on the Flight Simulator, you battle to master the Battledroid.

Roll one dice and add the score to your pilot skill. Add 2 if you have Satellite-Informed Radar Scan.

*If the score is 12 or more, turn to **317**.*

*If the score is 11 or less, turn to **52**.*

95

The Probe glides undetected past the wheezing droid, and you guide it quickly up a steep, ribbed tubeway, which emerges in a high-roofed chamber. At the centre of the chamber, bathed in a cone of red light, stand a cluster of long-limbed transparent-skinned Fentusians. Through the joints of their bulky black space armour you can see green blood coursing through their exposed, swollen veins.

The Fentusians gaze with dark-hooded eyes at a white-haired man in scarlet crushed-velvet robes, who kneels at their centre. His face is covered by a black silk blindfold, and you notice that he wears a Transporter Bracelet on his wrist with the digits 231 displayed upon it.

You recognise one of the Fentusians by his pot-belly, trembling skull and shocking orange mane, as Death-General Violwart. He begins to speak, and the Probe-monitor's compuspeak system translates his words:

"So, Holy Emperor, you choose to p-p-plead for your p-p-precious galaxy's life with the great Overlord Maldraggon. Ha! Your ancient mind deludes you."

Dragging his captive to his feet, and dribbling uncontrollably, Violwart hisses, "Despatch him in the Black Widow Spider Droid, and cast his miserable body into the crimson lava-pools of Oric."

Having seen and heard enough, you guide the probe back to the Battledroid.

If you have a Manually-Operated Shuttle and wish to pilot it into the Wolf Tower tunnel to your left, turn to **293**.

If you wish to await the flight of the Spider Droid, turn to **303**.

96

Your stomach lurches as a blast from the Trucker's parachute-pods slows it suddenly down to sub-light speed. Through the spaceship's screen you see the smooth, bright yellow surface of a small planet, and your pilot announces huskily: "We have reached the planet Zol, last outpost of Caluphex." Beyond Zol, you can see the first wisps of white mist that mark the beginning of the poorly-charted Fentusian Gulf.

If you are travelling in Space Trucker Alpha, turn to **265**.

If you are travelling in Space Trucker Beta, turn to **177**.

If you are travelling in Space Trucker Gamma, turn to **145**.

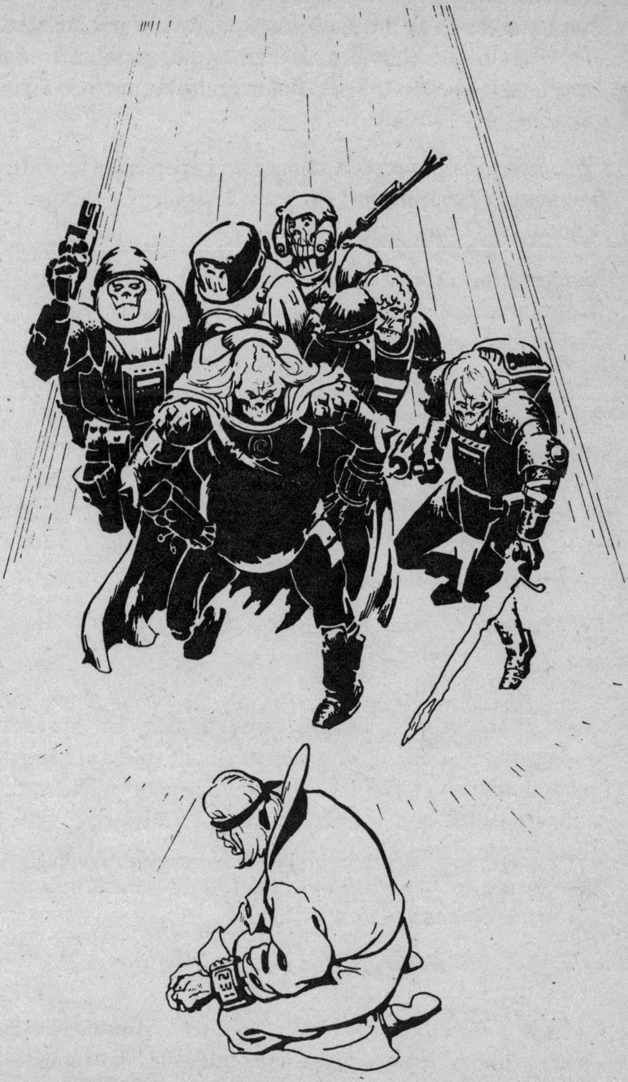

97

The Battledroid's Human-Reaction Sensors cause it to reel around and flinch as the Lava Beast attacks venomously with teeth, tusks and its fiery breath. Fighting desperately to ward off the attack, you pass your palm over the Automated Claw's bio-reader.

If you wish to grasp the hulking Lava Beast with your Automated Claw, turn to 129.

If you wish to snatch the tiny Flame Drake from his perch on the Lava Beast's back, turn to 233.

98

After three kilometres, the causeway divides into two, and from one of its forks a Hover-Droid speeds towards you, piloted by the tiny, fur-covered frame of a Flame Drake. It has no attack facilities, but trusts to its astonishing speed for defence, as it darts in to examine the Battledroid. A Fire and Ice Jet work facility hangs at its side.

If you have Gamma-Wave Intercom and the Droid Master's Symbol, turn to 287.

If you do not have both these items, the Flame Drake speeds away, leaving you to select a path.

If you wish to go south according to micro-compass readings, turn to 169.

If you wish to go west according to micro-compass readings, turn to 18.

99

If you are travelling by Hover, deduct 2 from your laser reserves. The tubeway emerges in a huge circular room, filled with animated hologram-discs, operated by Robotrons whose programming is insufficient to recognise you as an intruder. The discs vividly depict a Mutant-Spore crashing into an avenue approaching Anthracitex-9 SpaceDrome. The glass orb smashes on the steel avenue, scattering Hover-Bugs about it, and releasing a reptilian Flesh Mutant, its foul body bathed in a putrid slime. Maldraggon's evil host are clearly nearer than you thought.

If you have a Mutant Sensory Unit, you may be able to obtain vital information from the hologram-discs. The Securi-Pod, though, has settled on a landing-pad, and its doors are slowly lowering for the Rockworm crew to disembark.

If you have a Mutant Sensory Unit and wish to activate it, turn to 57.

If you do not have this facility, or would prefer to escape through the portal in the far side of the room, turn to 130.

100

You guide the Battledroid quickly across the vast marble platform, avoiding the numerous small droids that rush about their various tasks and duties.

Twelve huge light-bridges reach out from the marble dais, alongside their respective docking bays. In three of these huge rectangular docks rest the 800-metre long Dragon-Class Space Truckers, their fat bellies floating gently on the laser-light. Even in the Battledroid you feel dwarfed by these great craft. Their sleek hulls are adorned with sweeping areo-foil wings and massive ignition chambers and rocket pods. They rest on top of the deep-breasted, square cargo-holds which lie with their portals opened against the light-bridges. Their control turrets rest on the long, thin prows that gave the Dragon-Class Space Truckers their name. Turn to **154**.

101

Thrusting the Battledroid forward, you travel out on to the lava plateau, stopping abruptly when a huge geyser erupts from the ground only metres ahead of you.

If you wish to continue across the lava plateau, turn to **242**.

If you wish to guide the Battledroid down into the darkness of the geyser's enormous blow-hole, turn to **132**.

102

You engage the Fire and Ice Jet, and it emerges from its facility socket. Clasping its controls, you guide the jet down to the mercury-lift. The computer, impersonating your voice-pattern, quietly asks you, "Fire or ice, Battledroid pilot?"

If you wish to launch a cone of fire at the silver disc, turn to **22**.

If you wish to launch a cone of ice at the silver disc, turn to **291**.

103

Back in the Battledroid's control tower, you instruct the computer to transfer your Craft Master's gifts from the Shuttle's Matter Receptacle to your turret. They immediately appear before you for examination. One is the famed AnthraSun, one of the twelve wonders of the galaxy – a chink of pure light encased in Anthracite. You insert it into a socket in your control panel: add 6 to your laser-banks maximum, and raise your laser reserves accordingly. The other item is a Mind Choker, which links your pulse with that of your Craft Master when placed around your neck. In times of dire need, you may now telepathically contact your Craft Master. Note both items on your Status Chart.

If you wish to head east, turn to **214**.

If you wish to head north, turn to **142**.

104

The Battledroid's sniffer-probes extend from its stomach and investigate the debris. They open an old Torch-Bearer droid's storage hold, and three crystals tumble out. One has a small diamond encrusted at its centre, one a buckled gold coin, and one a rusted silver coin. The Battledroid's standard-grab transfers the crystals into its Matter Receptacle, in a hatch in its chest.

The probes also uncover a Fire and Ice Jet work facility, made weightless by an anti-gravity field which activates as the prod touches it. You may attach this facility to the Battledroid, with no addition of extra weight. (Note any items you take on your Status Chart.)

You guide the Battledroid into a tunnel descending steeply from the north of the chamber. Turn to **253**.

105

After some three kilometres, your scanners detect two craft, locked in combat. As you get closer, the Battledroid's Image-Enhancer displays a curious picture. A droid with enormously long legs, equipped with a Fire and Ice Jet work facility and piloted by a small grey-furred Flame Drake, has a large automaton clasped in its automated claw facility. The automaton, an unpiloted droid, has a large green M embossed on its hull, and an enormous rotor-blade spinning above its head. The two droids are battling furiously, both fighting with the flourescent snaking tongues of laser whips.

If you wish to go to Flame Drake's aid, turn to **239**.

If you wish to join the automated droid in attacking the Flame Drake, turn to **190**.

If you wish to ignore the robotic combatants, turn to **64**.

106

The Battledroid plummets over the end of the light-bridge and, before you can engage Hover mode, pitches into the SpaceDrome's energy bay, a pool of pure laser-power. For a split-second you glance up at the Rockworms' twisted faces gazing down from the brink of the light-bridge. Then there is a blinding flash, and your life is over.

107

As the portal slides open, you guide the Shuttle into a large high-roofed chamber, at the far end of which stand a cluster of long-limbed, transparent-skinned Fentusians, clad in bulky black space armour. They are waiting to ascend a "ladder of light" – an anti-gravity elevator – into the belly of the Black Widow Spider Droid which clings to a transparent spire high above you.

As the last of the Fentusians, clad in a heavy black robe, begins his ascent, he pauses and turns, his dark-hooded eyes sweeping the room. You recognise the trembling, pot-bellied figure of the flame-haired Death-General Violwart. Upon seeing the Shuttle, he raises his arm and launches a rough-hewn chunk of metal from a wrist-cannon. It seems to swell and metamorphose as it hurtles towards you, transforming rapidly into a deadly Droid-Falcon. You grasp the combat controls as the Droid-Falcon's carbonite-tipped claws rake the Shuttle's screen centimetres from your face. (Range = 0)

DROID-FALCON: Attack = 12 Defence = 5 Absorption = 1 Laser Reserves = 11.

If you destroy the Droid-Falcon, turn to **84**.

108

As you drift through the mists, you ask your computer for any relevant information. On the viewing screen, it prints up the following simple message: "Fentusian Gulf: poorly charted region separating Caluphex and Fentusia Galaxies. Comprised of highly unstable, inflammable gas clouds."

Suddenly, an alarm whistles through your control turret, and a small craft appears on the Battledroid's viewing screen, emerging from the mist. Its short, fat hull is peppered with rust, black smoke billows from its long-outdated nuclear engines, and a tangled nest of multi-coloured wires trails from its belly. The ramshackle craft, some relic of a bygone age, limps towards you, its ancient cannon-ports lowered and aimed in your direction.

If you have a Gamma-Wave Intercom and wish to contact the craft's pilot, turn to **211**.

If you do not have this facility, or wish only to defend yourself, turn to **3**.

109

As you enter the Metropolis, a strange craft swoops down towards you from the roof of a massive crystal tower. The craft is a Techno-Leach, constructed from thousands of protoplastic bubbles, each filled with sensors and probes. In a large bubble at the craft's centre sits a Flame Drake, weakly manipulating its controls. The Techno-Leach soars down and hits the Battledroid's hull with a dull plop, attaching itself solidly. Your computer screen instantly goes blank, and the Battledroid fails to respond to your controls. The Techno-Leach grows red, as if sucking out the Battledroid's lifeblood. Deduct 2 from your computer capacity.

*If you wish to engage attack facilities, turn to **222**.*

*If you wish to deactivate the Battledroid's computer and switch to manual control, turn to **82**.*

110

The roadway widens out to join hundreds of others in a huge avenue crafted from polished steel. A heat haze shimmers over it as thousands of craft head north towards the SpaceDrome, in desperate flight from their doomed planet. Turn to **292**.

111

The Fentusian leaps forward and strikes viciously with his laser sword once more, cackling and spitting. Roll one dice, and deduct 2 from the score if you are wearing space armour. Deduct the total from your life force.

If you still live, you level the Molecular Disruptor at the Fentusian and reduce his grotesque body to dust.

Muttering a silent prayer of thanks for your miraculous survival, you re-activate the Battledroid. It shudders, bursts into life, then tears itself free from the grip of the abandoned Scout-Wasp. Turn to **299**.

112

The tubeway emerges after a short distance in a narrow, stone-walled chamber. As you enter, a large robotron, clumsily attired in a flowing white robe, totters towards you, chattering:

"Welcome to the Droid Master's chambers ... Please be prepared to present jubilee crystals... have you permission to be here....where are the Tuskquartz miners....the Master does not like to be disturbed ... who are you .....?"

The robotron has no attack facilities and so poses no threat to the Battledroid. It does, though, have a Tuskquartz Orb attached to its neck, a facility capable of recharging your laser banks at regular intervals. It is surrounded by the blue glow of an anti-gravity field, indicating that it is weightless.

If you wish to ignore the robotron and exit through a tubeway heading north, turn to 8.

If you have an Automated Claw, and wish to steal the Tuskquartz Orb, roll one dice, and add 1 to the score if your computer capacity is 12 or over.

If the score is 3 or less, turn to 32.

If the score is 4 or more, turn to 283.

113

The pilot activates the glowing jettison bio-reader, and the Battledroid drifts out into Space, its laser-banks throbbing as you re-engage them. The Trucker with the hawk on its hull opens its cargo-bay portals invitingly.

If you wish to guide the Battledroid into the Space Trucker, turn to 51.

If you wish to attack the Space Trucker, turn to 206.

114

You thrust the Battledroid up into the air as the seething plateau collapses into a wide crater. Running along the crater's base is the bottom of a broad tunnel, heading down into Oric's heart. The planet's unstable surface has been stirred into lethal activity by the might of the fire-storm, and glancing back at the livid, purple sky, you seek sanctuary in the tunnel. Turn to 126.

115

The tubeway soon emerges in a huge chamber, the floor of which is constantly revolving and tilting. It is filled with the pounding pistons of an enormous, primitive machine, and in the dimness you can also sense a brooding presence. Touching the controls, you flood the chamber with brilliant light from the Battledroid's megawatt floodlights, to reveal a creature from your worst nightmares.

A grotesque mutant wearing a spiked collar rears up on its hind legs at the centre of the chamber. Its bloated belly lies in great folds of flesh on the cold steel floor, and its thin, spined legs rock with the motion of the tilting room. Its leathery tail, patched with blotches of white fungus, is entwined around the chamber, choking the machinery where it is enmeshed in the thrusting pistons.

Although the frail leg of its last victim still dangles from the mutant's mouth, it does not hesitate to slope hungrily towards you, an atom-blaster clasped in its claw. (Range: 200m)

ORICAN GUARDIAN MUTANT: Attack = 14 Defence = 5 Absorption = 4 Life Reserves = 15 (Gain Bonus for Negative-Ion Flame Thrower) (Immune to Nuclear Jet)

If you win, there is a portal leading from the north wall of the chamber. Turn to **230**.

116

Deduct 2 from your laser-banks if travelling by Hover.

You gaze at the hypnotic images of the rolling blood-red clouds, before thrusting the Battledroid into a tubeway heading north. Turn to **314**.

117

The Shuttle's claw depresses the green button with a dull click. There is silence. Then the Limpet Droid falls harmlessly away from the Battledroid, and drifts off into Space. The "G" stands for the Fentusian '*gazith*', meaning "stop", and marked the

Limpet Droid's emergency deactivating button. You disable its deadly partner in the same way, then guide the Shuttle back into the coasting Battledroid. Turn to **290**.

118

Your Matter Transporter Pod shimmers as millions of particles gradually form into a single entity within it. To your horror, the figure that gradually appears is a gangling, milky-skinned Fentusian stormtrooper, clad in black space armour. He clutches a three-bladed laser-sword and stares at you through dark-hooded eyes with a hatred that chills your heart. As he completes his reformation, you fumble desperately for some means of defence.

If you have a digi-ring and wish to twist it to the right, turn to **176**.

If you have a Molecular Disruptor and wish to level it at the Fentusian, roll one dice and add 2 to the score if your pilot skill is 10 or more, but deduct 1 if wearing space armour:-

If the total is 4 or more, turn to **176**.

If the total is 3 or less, turn to **268**.

If you have neither of these items, turn to **205**.

119

For three days you speed through the galaxy in the belly of the great Space Trucker. Bouts of light-speed flight are broken up by long, slow stretches of sub-light travel, to negotiate asteroid belts and reserve the Trucker's Tuskquartz fuel.

Your head aches from lack of sleep and the constant throbbing of the Trucker's laser-banks, and you reach for another handful of zincite capsules to nourish you and ward off the crippling effects of space-sickness. Shade in three days on your Status Chart.

The Trucker suddenly shudders as it emerges from the dazzling tunnel of light-speed once more. This time, though, the dark blanket of space is broken by a large, green planet, filling the Trucker's viewing screen. The pilot announces that he is docking to recharge his engines, and to request computer-charts for the Fentusian Gulf. Turn to **297**.

120

As you emerge into the chamber, the senses of the Battledroid seem to become dulled. Your vision through the viewing screen becomes blurred, the throb of your electron-pulse engines becomes distant, and your movements slow.

You realise that the giant compartment is filled with a dense blue liquid. It clogs the Battledroid's air-filters and a red alert message from the computer screams: "Life-support systems will shut down after 5,000 millisecs!"

The compartment is completely spherical, and the Battledroid, its gyro-sensors shuddering to keep balance, keeps sliding down towards the lowest point:

If you have an Auxiliary Oxygen Supply and wish to activate it, turn to 217.

If you wish to allow the Battledroid to float gently to the bottom of the globe, turn to 171.

If you wish to thrust the Battledroid up towards the ceiling of the chamber, turn to 276.

If you wish to thrust the Battledroid towards the far side of the chamber, turn to 312.

121

Two white laser beams scream from the nose of the sleek, black fighter and, with a blinding flash of light, slam into your turret. Roll one dice to assess damage to your laser-banks, and two dice to determine where the Battledroid has been hit. If you have a defence facility in this area, deduct its absorption from the damage.

You are momentarily blinded by the explosion of the lasers, recovering your sight only to see the Space Fighter closing for the kill. You must fight for your life. (Range = 1km)

FENTUSIAN SPACE FIGHTER: Attack = 13 Defence = 6 Absorption = 2 Laser Reserves = 10 (Gain Bonus for Laser-Bomb Launcher) (Immune to Negative-Ion Flame Thrower)

If you defeat the Space Fighter, turn to 94.

122

You approach the force-gate in the wake of a huge, tarnished green Viper-Coaster, its multi-jointed body filled with centuries old radioactive waste. As it snakes along, high above the roadway, the force-gate's Rockworm guard thrusts his twisted claw into the bio-reader beside him. The shimmering blue rays instantly descend from the red vapour above you, and disappear into the launcher submerged in the granite path. The Viper-Coaster is so large that you may be able to follow it through the forces-gate, for no guard would launch the electric beams while a waste-carrier was in their path.

If you wish to select Hover mode and travel through the force-gate above the Viper-Coaster, turn to **31**.

If you wish to thrust the Battledroid through the force-gate below the Viper-Coaster, turn to **304**.

If you would prefer to follow the pathway around to the east, where another force-gate and its Rockworm guard blocks the path, turn to **81**.

123

You master the Battledroid and guide it gently down to Oric's surface. You land at the centre of a grey causeway of solidified lava, which cuts through a crimson sea of bubbling molten lava. Add 2 to your pilot skill.

If your Time-Chart shows seven days or more, turn to **92**.

If your Time-Chart shows six days or less, turn to **299**.

124

The Battledroid's standard probe-lever grasps the silver crystal from its Matter Holder, and presses it gently into the crystal-receiver. A burst of flame shoots from the receiver, and the portal explodes. Roll two dice and deduct the score from your laser-banks. If you survive, you retrieve the crystal from the portal's remains and thrust the Battledroid on down the tubeway. Turn to **278**.

125

The Rockworms, their eyes wide in amazement as they gaze up at the towering Battledroid, stand aside at the sign of the Drome Master. You guide the great craft forward on to the light-bridge and across to the Docking Hangar. Turn to **311**.

126

You descend into a huge horizontal tunnel, its dusty white walls eerily illuminated by torches thrust into rusted iron holders. The Battledroid's scanners reveal no life-force close by, and the tunnel echoes emptily.

*If you wish to head north according to micro-compass readings, turn to **16**.*

*If you wish to head south according to micro-compass readings, turn to **305**.*

127

You pass your hand over the Battledroid's Trucker-Link bio-reader, and your control turret extends forward into the Space Trucker's Droid-Link. As it settles into this 30-metre socket, two steel shutters slide apart and a glass viewing tunnel reveals the Space Trucker's control room; allowing you to see through the Trucker's viewing screen.

Your captain is seated in a large pilot couch, his back towards you. Over the Droid-Link, you explain that you wish to be taken to Oric.

The pilot replies, "Oric is beyond normal Trucker routes. Do you wish me to follow the Delta-3 or Delta-6 ley-line?"

*If you wish the Trucker to follow the Delta-3 ley-line, turn to **267**.*

*If you wish the Trucker to follow the Delta-6 ley-line, turn to **20**.*

128

As the probe-lever inserts the diamond crystal, the crystal-receiver melts as if touched with acid, and the portal explodes. Roll two dice and deduct the score from your laser banks.

If you still survive, thrust the Battledroid on along the tubeway, after retrieving the crystal from the debris. Turn to **315**.

129

The Automated Claw shoots forward and pierces the Lava Beast's flesh with its sharp fingers. The creature bellows in agony, and rears up on its hind legs. The Automated Claw is torn from the Battledroid, still embedded in the Lava Beast's side, its wiring torn out. Remove this facility from your Status Chart.

The Lava Beast continues its attack with renewed fury. Turn back to **246** and fight to the death.

130

You thrust the Battledroid into the centre of a poorly lit, echoing room: the Entrance Bay of Anthracitex-9 SpaceDrome. It is empty but for the SpaceDrome's guardian, the Drome Master; an official renowned for his honesty and intelligence. This tiny creature sits cross-legged inside, and controls, a small, tumbling, transparent orb known as a Drome-Walker, through which shoot tiny flecks of light. Like an insect buzzing around the Battledroid, the Drome-Walker flits about the huge chamber with astonishing speed. Suddenly it stops, and floats gently up to the level of your control turret, the apparently weightless Drome Master somersaulting forward to face you. Through the misted orb you can see the large, sharp-tipped ears and doleful, staring eyes of this goblin-like creature.

If you killed a Rockworm earlier in your adventure, turn to **256**.

If you did not, turn to **35**.

131

The two Fentusians, one stormtrooper and one battle-marshall, burst into your turret, swinging their three-bladed laser swords wildly. Their skin is transparent, revealing their pumping hearts and the coursing of green blood through their swollen veins. You see the muscles of the Fentusians' gangling bodies contract violently as they raise their laser swords to strike you down in cold blood.

If you have a digi-ring and wish to turn it to the right, turn to 23.

If you have a digi-ring and wish to turn it to the left, turn to 270.

If you have a Molecular Disruptor and wish to open fire, turn to 196.

If you have neither of these items, or wish to trust to Fentusian mercy, turn to 205.

132

As the great fountain of water descends back into the geyser you guide the Battledroid down into the gaping blow-hole. You emerge in an underground lake, bubbling and boiling with heat. The water gurgles in your air-filters, as they struggle to extract sufficient oxygen to maintain your life-support systems.

If you have an Auxiliary Oxygen Supply, turn to 245.

If you do not, turn to 28.

133

You press your palm against the bio-reader below the Independent Information Probe's info-panel, and watch as the transparent sphere drifts slowly away from the Battledroid. Your pilot couch elevates several metres until you are positioned within the circular console of the control turret computer facility. A glass screen encircling your head depicts a

360° image of the Information Probe's infra-camera pictures, and transmits every sound recorded by its Micro-Bug Sensors. A remote-control column descends from the console, and grasping it you guide the Probe into the shaft. Turn to **204**.

134

As the Spider Droid soars towards you, the Battledroid's Image Enhancer reveals its two pilots. One has the typical transparent flesh of the Fentusians, but it is not taut, hanging instead in gruesome, green-veined folds. His face is twisted, and his bright red lips quiver. His twitching co-pilot is squat and heavily armoured, with a shock of orange hair falling from his jerking, snuffling head. From the Galactic Gazette Holograms of Horror, you recognise these creatures as the evil Fentusian Overlord Maldraggon and his simpering side-kick, Death-General Violwart. (Range = 500m)

FENTUSIAN SPIDER DROID: Attack = 15 Defence = 8 Absorption = 2 Laser Reserves = 18 (Gain Bonus for Laser Port) (Immune to Psi-Exuder)

*If you defeat the Fentusian Spider Droid, turn to **285**.*

135

You press your hand against the flame-thrower's bio-reader, and a computer-guided jet of flame shoots from the attack facility. The flames seem to catch on the highly unstable, inflammable mists of the Fentusian Gulf. There is a thunderous roar, and a huge fireball engulfs the Battledroid. Your mission is over, commemorated only by the inter-galactic fire which will burn in the gulf for many years.

136

The passageway descends for several hundred metres before sweeping round and climbing once more. It eventually comes

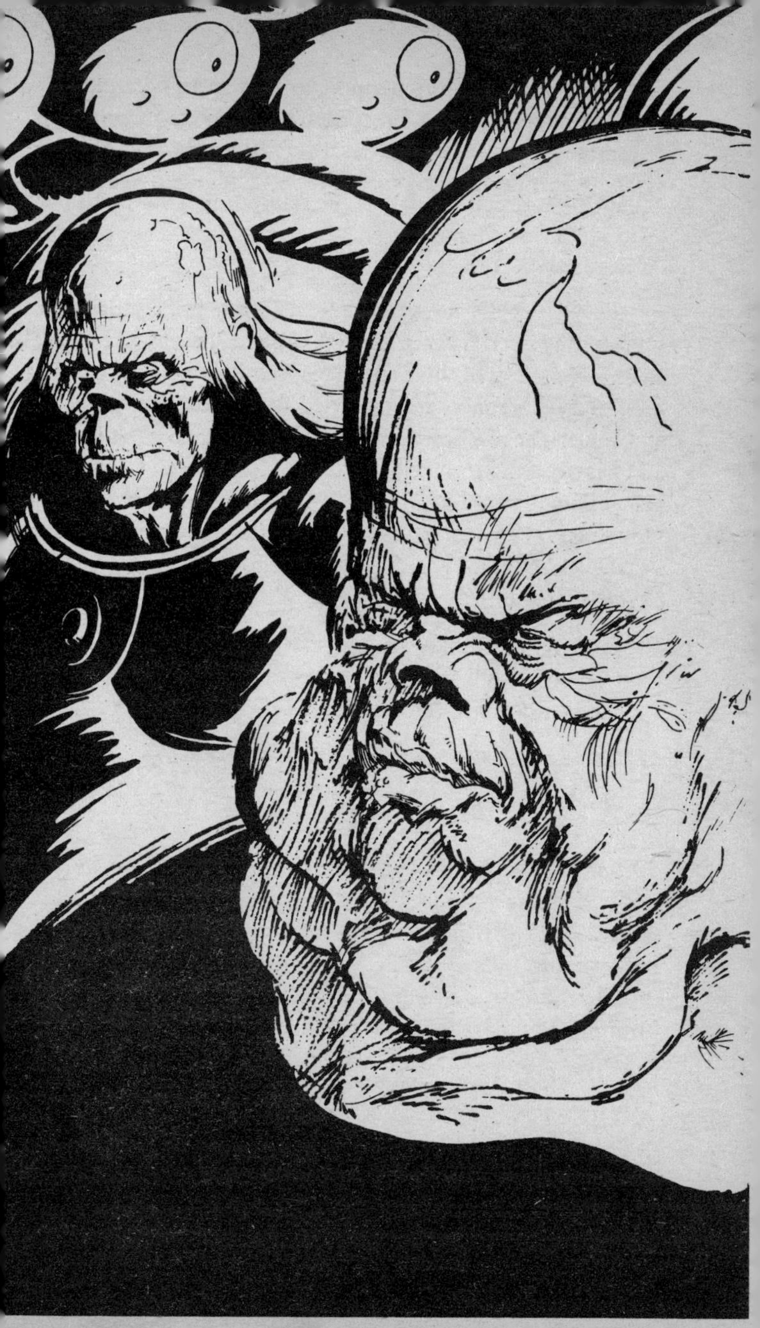

to a portal of wavering white light, which seems to suck the Battledroid towards it. You pass through the portal into a passageway.

Glancing through the rear of the Battledroid's viewing screen, you see the portal has vanished, replaced by a smoothly mined wall. Turn to **70**.

137

The Mutant-Spore shatters on the steel roadway, its passenger tumbling out and unfurling its long wet body. Flourishing a laser whip in one of its many hands and spitting acid from its gaping mouth, the Flesh Mutant lunges towards the Battledroid. (Range = 50m)

FLESH MUTANT: Attack = 10 Defence = 7 Absorption = 1 Life Reserves = 14 (Gain Bonus for Laser Port) (Immune to Rotary Laser-Bomb Launcher)

If you win, turn to **263**.

138

As the Battledroid strides to the left of the robo-mutant, the creature squeals with delight. Grasping your control turret with its left claw, the robo-mutant has plenty of room to flail the whip against you, its laser-tips bursting into metallic flame as they strike your defence shields. (Range = 50m)

ROBO-MUTANT: Attacks = 15 Defence = 7 Absorption = 2 Laser Reserves = 13 (Gain Bonus for Laser Port) (Immune to Rotary Laser-Bomb Launcher)

If you defeat the robo-mutant, you exit from the cavern through a small, sliding portal in its southern wall. Turn to **68**.

139

The Lava Louse does not attempt to attack the Battledroid, but concentrates instead on forcing its formless body through your viewing screen. It ignores your attacks, though the Psi-Exuder clearly hurts it. Fight it as normal, but begin every combat round at stage 10. (Range = 0)

LAVA LOUSE: Attack = 0 Defence = 5 Absorption = 2 Life Reserves = 30 (Gain Bonus for Psi-Exuder) (Immune to all other weapons)

If you fail to kill the Lava Louse after 3 combat rounds, turn to **174**.

If you defeat the Lava Louse, turn to **101**.

140

The Radar Scan guides you slowly along the Alpha-2 ley-line as you progress deeper and deeper into the gulf. Shade in three days on your Status Chart and turn to **108**.

141

The 200-metre tall Battledroid's powerful progress disturbs the heavy flagstones and jolts them out of place. Their movement reveals the dark sewer tunnel running beneath the Metropolis. To your horror, an enormous mutated head emerges slowly from the sewer, slime and filth sliding from its bald, brown-boned skull. With a hiss, it attacks the Battledroid. (Range = 500m)

SEWER BEAST: Attack = 14 Defence = 3 Absorption = 4 Laser Reserves = 20 (Gain Bonus for Laser Port, Rotary Laser-Bomb Launcher) (Immune to Sonic Punch)

*If you defeat the Sewer Beast, continue along the roadway by turning to **318**.*

142

The Battledroid arrives at a junction, one tubeway heading east from another travelling north to south. A visual display unit indicates that the SpaceDrome Security Bay lies to the north, and the Holding Bay to the east.

*If you wish to head east, turn to **314**.*

*If you wish to follow the tubeway going north, turn to **76**.*

143

You pass your palm over the Master bio-reader, and the old man is flung clear by the Battledroid's defence shields, his body charred and ruined. A cone of flame erupts from the Battledroid's unfinished internal circuitry, and the Battledroid explodes.

The old man looks up from the wreckage and murmurs:

"There is evil abroad indeed, for this was not meant to be." Your mission is over.

144

You programme the north-west Hot Spring Plains co-ordinates into your flight-computer and thrust the Battledroid into Oric's atmosphere.

*If your Time-Chart shows seven days or more, turn to **223**.*

*If your Time-Chart shows six days or less, turn to **94**.*

145

The Trucker pilot swivels round on his pilot couch to face you. He eases his space helm off, to reveal the taut transparent skin, wide sunken eyes and slitted mouth of a Fentusian. From his tattered ears hang many golden earrings in the hawk design of a Space Pirate. He grins horribly at you, and through his clear skin you see the throbbing brain, pulsing veins and gnarled bones of his skull. "Welcome!" he spits, as his compatriots in the cargo-bay pods lower their concealed laser ports and open fire. The pirates are attacking from the rear. (Range = 100m)

FENTUSIAN SPACE PIRATES: Attack = 13 Defence = 9 Absorption = 2 Laser Reserves = 14 (Gain Bonus for Tail-Guard Disintegrator) (Immune to Nuclear Jet)

If you win, turn to **65**.

146

Fending off the Droid Master's Gladiator, the Battledroid destroys a bank of computer terminals to your left. As it does so, a jet of flame shoots down the Gladiator's umbilical control tube. The hulking automaton shudders, and its great legs collapse. Swinging from the charred control tube, the Gladiator continues to hold you with its pincer, but it seems now to swing its laser sword blindly. Begin a new combat round, using the figures below, and deducting any damage you have already inflicted from the automaton's laser reserves. (Range = 0)

DROID MASTER'S GLADIATOR: Attack = 11 Defence = 6 Absorption = 2 Laser Reserves = 15 − damage (Gain Bonus for Negative-Ion Flame Thrower, Sonic Punch: combine bonus if you have both.) (Immune to Psi-Exuder)

If you win, turn to **46**.

147

As you press on into the thronging SpaceDrome, you spy a small deactivated Servling Droid – a droid designed to carry out tasks for its master – being trampled underfoot. You dive down and recover it, discovering to your delight that it can be easily restored. Note Servling Droid on your Status Chart. Tucking your prize beneath your arm, you head back to the Space Trucker.

If you are travelling on Space Trucker Alpha or Space Trucker Beta, turn to 288.

If you are travelling on Space Trucker Gamma, turn to 71.

148

The Battledroid crashes into the webbing at the floor of the crevasse, catapulting a cloud of dust, droid debris and dried bones up into the cavern. A steel spike punctures the Battledroid's back as you hit the ground, throwing the squirming Crevasse Crawler clear. Deduct 1 from your attack capacity and roll one dice for damage to your laser-banks. If you are still alive, the Crevasse Crawler renews its frenzied attack. Deduct the damage you have already inflicted from its life reserves. (Range = 50m)

CREVASSE CRAWLER: Attack = 12 Defence = 7 Absorption = 1 Life Reserves = 25 – damage (Gain Bonus for Psi-Exuder) (Immune to Sonic Punch)

If you defeat the Crevasse Crawler, engage Hover mode and escape the cavern floor's groping shadows by thrusting the Battledroid back up to the silver platform. Turn to 150.

149

The Shuttle's claw depresses the red "S" button with a dull click. There is silence. Then there is a deafening explosion.

The "S" stands for the Fentusian "*serazith*", meaning "go", and marks the switch activating the Limpet Droid. Roll one dice and deduct the score from the Battledroid's laser banks. Your Shuttle is thrown clear of the Battledroid, and the gulf's mists engulf you momentarily before you find your way back to your mother ship. You depress the green switch on the second Limpet Droid, and it drifts harmlessly into Space, as you guide the Shuttle back to its facility holder. Turn to **290**.

150

The Battledroid stands on a large transparent circular disc, containing a metallic silver liquid, set into the causeway. Your computer identifies it as a moveable glass platform covering a deep column of mercury.

*If you wish to head south, turn to **259**.*

*If you have an "a" beside your computer capacity and wish to consult your computer, turn to **307**.*

*If you have an Automated Claw and wish to use it in an attempt to move the mercury-filled glass column, turn to **6**.*

*If you have a Sonic Punch and wish to use it in an attempt to move the mercury-filled glass column, turn to **75**.*

*If you have a Fire and Ice Jet, and wish to use it in an attempt to move the mercury column, turn to **102**.*

*If you have a Negative-Ion Flame Thrower and wish to use it in an attempt to move the mercury column, turn to **22**.*

151

After some thirty minutes, your pilot re-emerges in the Trucker's control turret, a bottle of the powerful alcoholic drink, Gamma-Juice, clutched tightly in one hand. He sits heavily in his pilot couch and, murmuring "prepare for light-speed engagement", thrusts the Space Trucker's control column forward. Turn to **14**.

152

The Battledroid's Matter Transporter Pod vibrates as millions of particles shimmer into life within it and begin to take the shape of a humanoid. A small figure with a mane of snow white hair and wearing heavy scarlet robes gradually appears. Stumbling from the Transporter Pod, he falls to his knees and speaks to you in a quavering voice:

"I am Vizo Rath, Holy Emperor of Anthracitex-9, Independent Overseer of Caluphex and heir to the Rath dynasty. You have plucked me from the jaws of death, and with all my tired heart, I thank you."

With Caluphex's leader safe, your quest may yet succeed. With him aboard, you have the key to unlock every Space Portal in the galaxy.

Vizo Rath recognizes Gan Tamil-Rath's Soul Server reclining in a passenger pod, but as he strides forward to greet him, the Battledroid suddenly shudders. The Black Widow Spider Droid has turned and launched a burst of laser bolts into your outer defence shields. Although you have discovered Gan Tamil-Rath, last of the Droid Masters, and rescued Holy Emperor Vizo Rath, only if you destroy the mighty Fentusian Spider Droid will your quest be complete. Turn to **62**.

153

The gaping jaws engulf you and the Battledroid into the belly of the massive robot. Over fifty Mutant Sensory Units line the robot's stomach, and they instantly start to sniff, scratch and taste the Battledroid.

The roar of the robot's Tuskquartz-boost engines deafens you for several minutes, and the Battledroid shakes violently as you are carried to your unknown destination.

Eventually the robot slows to a halt, and with a sudden blast of hot air, spits out the Battledroid. You stare about you in wonder at a sprawling Metropolis of huge mid-air buildings linked with twisting tubeways and laser rails. Glancing nervously back at the skulking robot, you proceed into the Metropolis. Turn to **178**.

154

The captains of the three ships stand beside their craft awaiting orders, and you must decide which of them will pilot you to the Fentusian Gulf.

The first Space Trucker, Dragon-Class Alpha, has much of its royal blue paint peeling off, and its cargo bay is peppered with the dents of numerous asteroid storms. Your image enhancer shows the pilot sitting with his back against the cargo-hold step. His leather space armour is crumpled and dirty, his long hair ruffled, and he sucks wearily at a stick of the stimulant known as Jethal-Bone.

The second Space Trucker, Dragon-Class Beta, is in spotless condition, its dark paintwork embellished with silver tracery. Its pilot stands proudly at the centre of the cargo doors, dressed in brightly buffed laserite space armour. A helmet is clutched under his arm. He wears dark space-goggles, his hair is slicked back and you notice he has a gold tooth as he chews on a crumpled cigar.

The third Space Trucker, Dragon-Glass Gamma, is painted in matt black, but for an area of white paint daubed rudely on the side. It has extra rocket-pods and retracted facilities of some kind. The Trucker's captain wears full space armour under a heavy grey cloak, beneath which you notice the butt of

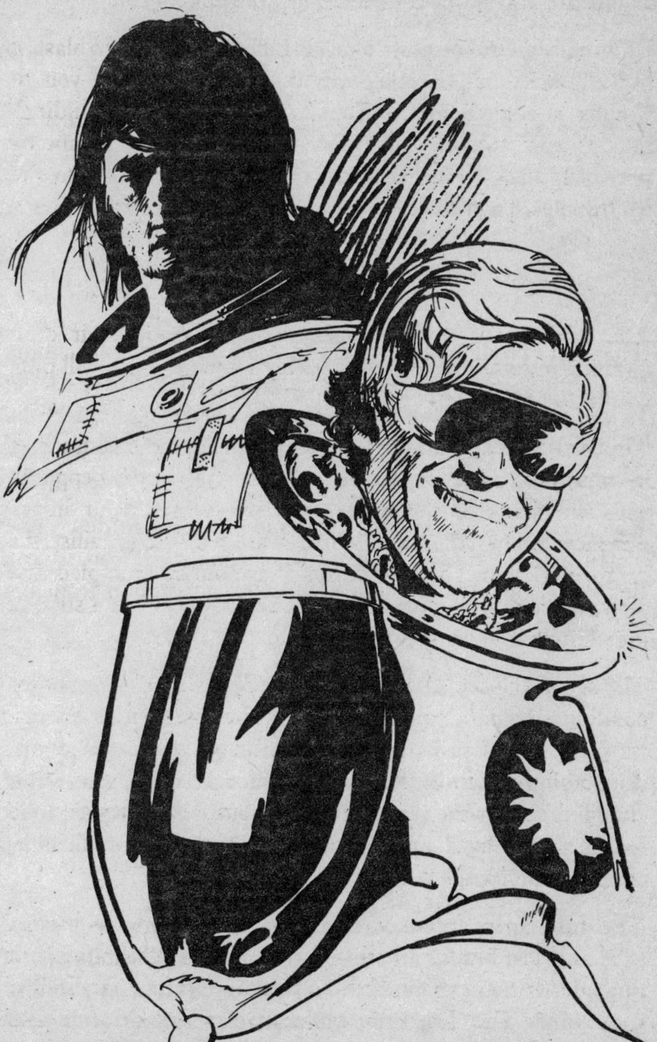

a laser blaster. He is wearing a dark-visored space-helm, and leans against the side of his cargo bay, glancing constantly about him.

If you wish to travel on Dragon-Class Trucker Alpha, turn to **308**.

If you wish to travel on Dragon-Class Trucker Beta, turn to **221**.

If you wish to travel on Dragon-Class Trucker Gamma, turn to **29**.

155

The Battledroid's attack facilities have no chance of halting the lightning-fast missile. Their activity merely increases the Battledroid's heat, and presents an easier target for the torpedo's heat sensors. The missile slams into the Battledroid with a deafening roar.

Roll two dice to assess damage, and two dice to determine which area of the Battledroid has been hit. If you have a defence facility in this area, deduct its absorption from the damage.

If the Battledroid is still functioning, turn to **225**.

156

The hulking Battledroid springs into the pool, splattering pink liquid over the plexoglass walls, and is submerged to its waist. Your digi-displays indicate that all combat facilities remain functional.

The automaton attacks with its armoury of photon-phasers, plus a special attack. After every combat round, it spits a jet of pink fluid at your control turret, severely reducing visibility. You must deduct 1 from your attack capacity after each round, for the duration of this combat: (Range = 200m)

TADPOLE II NEON SECURITY AUTOMATON: Attack = 12 Defence = 7 Absorption = 1 Laser Reserves = 17 (Gain Bonus for Sonic Punch, Rotary Laser-Bomb Launcher) (Immune to Nuclear Jet)

If you defeat the Tadpole Droid, thrust the Battledroid up through the 300-metre wide spiralling glass tubeway. Turn to **38**.

157

The Trucker swoops beneath Ironis-2, circles the planet once, then sweeps around on to a route identified by your computer as the Alpha-2 ley-line. Your pilot draws his communicator down to his mouth and asks in a hoarse whisper: "Do you wish to follow Alpha-2 or Delta-2, Battledroid pilot?"

If you wish to continue along the Alpha-2 ley-line, turn to **244**.

If you wish the Trucker to sweep around on to the Delta-2 ley-line, turn to **191**.

158

Clasping the controls of the probe-lever, you pluck the diamond-crystal from the Battledroid's Matter Holder and guide it into the crystal-receiver. The portal swings silently open, and the diamond-crystal is ejected on the tubeway's glass floor. After replacing it in the Matter Holder, you urge the Battledroid on down the tubeway. Turn to **298**.

159

As you plunge down towards Oric in the grasp of the Scout-Wasp, the laser tracery of a computer-coded message suddenly animates your viewing screen:

"Encoded Distress Call: – Source Code: Vizo Rath, Holy Emperor of Anthracitex-9, Overseer of Caluphex. Message: On mercy mission to Oric. Betrayed by Maldraggon. I am besieged. Please assist. End."

Your enemy is close at hand, and the sole heir to the Rath Dynasty is in his evil clutches. Vizo Rath's voice-pattern and palm-print unlock all Security Portals and Space Gates throughout the galaxies, so his rescue is now a vital part of your mission. The Battledroid's sensory-scan looks into his life force and duplicates the thud of his heartbeat over the audio-transmitters, so that you will know if his life is taken. Turn to **282**.

160

There is a blinding flash of light as your attack screams over the Aero-Limo's control turret, rocking the craft and searing the paint from its hydrofoil wings. Glancing at the viewing disc in your control tower, you see the Rockworm pilot flinch in a spasm of fear. He thrusts stumpy, wart-ridden fingers into a bio-reader beside him, and a Travel Crystal, reduced to tiny particles and beamed across a Matter Transporter, emerges from the control desk in front of you. Make a note of this in the space marked "Items" on your Status Chart, and add 2 to your computer capacity.

You thrust the Battledroid forward towards the electric force-gate, which is manned by a Rockworm, several hundred metres in front of you. Turn to **81**.

161

The pink anti-gravity gas has made the Battledroid weightless, and as you fire your attack facilities towards the floor, you simply thrust the Battledroid up into the portal's grey wash of light.

The Battledroid is instantly sucked into a turret of blinding brightness. Images of rearing Lava Beasts, fragile Flame Drakes, magnificent, soaring droids, and the crimson surface of Oric flash past you. The old man disappears into the distance behind you, but you can hear his distant voice, booming and echoing.

"Our life is but a journey through encounters which fly with purpose towards us. If our path is reversed we may travel back along our life-way. I have mastered Time, and can weave it. My Time-Warp Pool has thrust you back in time, cast you to an earlier moment in your life, that you may begin again . . ."

Earlier in your quest, you were instructed to note down the details of your Status Chart. Adjust your Status Chart so that it again reads exactly as it did then, removing any Items you have subsequently gained. The Battledroid emerges in the Fentusian Gulf at a point earlier in Time. Turn to **290**.

162

The causeway runs for several kilometres through the crimson sea, which lazily spits lumps of molten lava up at you that flame briefly as they strike the Battledroid's outer shields. Eventually the causeway divides into two.

If you wish to head east according to your micro-compass, turn to **18**.

If you wish to head south according to your micro-compass, turn to **273**.

If you have a Mutant Sensory Unit and wish to activate it, turn to **213**.

163

You drift on through the Fentusian Gulf until the Battledroid's computer suddenly bursts into life. It announces in a voice-pattern identical to your own: "The planet Oric, 602,431 milliseconds away, is locked into computer-sensor tracking device."

With a rush of excitement, you demand all information relating to Oric from the Battledroid's data-banks. A shimmering hologram appears on your viewing disc, showing Oric, a tiny crimson planet, orbiting a large marbled grey planet, Zzyus, to which it is linked by long red laser-rails cutting through Space. The computer slowly recites all its data on Oric:

"The planet Oric is so tiny that it registers as a slow-moving ship on many radar. It has a magnetic pole in the south — affecting compasses accordingly — and its surface is covered with searing-hot smouldering lava beds.

"Oric's heart is honeycombed with tunnels and huge, illuminated tubeways constructed to mine the precious laser-fuel, Tuskquartz. Neon laser-rails stretch from Oric to Zzyus, where merchants once traded diamonds and spices for Tuskquartz in a sprawling metropolis.

"Tuskquartz was hauled to Zzyus by caravans of lumbering Lava Beasts with their frail, telepathic masters, the Flame Drakes, mounted in turrets on their mighty backs. When the mines became exhausted Oric and Zzyus were abandoned. The forgotten Lava Beasts and Flame Drakes were left to forage desperately across Oric's desolate surface, and grew ferociously hostile.

"Legends tell that the Droid Master Gan Tamil-Rath settled on Oric in 3050 A.D. and tamed its inhabitants. Some records say that he lives on, crafting a machine to carry him back in time, protected by the Lava Beasts and a multitude of magnificent machines."

If you have reached Oric in five days, turn to **269**.

If you have reached Oric in six–nine days, turn to **306**.

If you have reached Oric in ten days, turn to **45**.

164

You launch a sniffer-prod from the Battledroid to investigate the careering robotron. As the prod touches it, the frantic droid spins around to face you, vibrates violently, then collapses in a heap, its head rolling from its shoulders. The robotron's storage-hold portal swings open to reveal three crystals. One has a diamond set in its centre, another a rusted silver coin, and the third a tarnished gold coin. The Battledroid's standard grab reaches out and transfers the crystals to your own Matter Holder. (Note them on your Status Chart.)

The robotron also has a Fire and Ice Jet work facility, made weightless by an anti-gravity pack. You may attach the Fire and Ice Jet to the Battledroid without adding any weight.

A steeply descending tunnel heads south from the chamber. Turn to **203**.

165

The Battledroid's throbbing engines power you quickly to within metres of the Aero-Limo as it glides smoothly along above the roadway. As the Battledroid's image-enhancer transmits an enlarged picture to your computer screen, you can see that at the rear of the craft sits a small man richly attired in scarlet robes. At the Aero-Limo's helm squats a hulking Rockworm, his blue-veined arms tattooed with many badges of service. He turns to look at you in horror, and wrestles with his craft's controls to steer it from the Battledroid's path.

*If you have Gamma-Wave Intercom and wish to contact the Aero-Limo, turn to **241**.*

*If you do not have this facility, or would prefer to give this official space-vehicle a wide berth, turn to **74**.*

166

The Flame Drake switches on his intercom and your compuspeak system translates his words, which are spoken in a beautiful, soothing language:

"I thank you for your help, Caluphexian. Our aims are as one. Maldraggon skulks in the Wolf Tower, torturing your Emperor Vizo Rath, who trembles in his scarlet mantle and tears at his snow white hair. If you wish to find my master, Gan Tamil-Rath, head for the Metropolis and seek the entrance to the deepest, darkest cave." Add 2 to your computer capacity.

If you wish to head in the direction indicated by the Flame Drake, south on your micro-compass, turn to **18**.

If you wish to follow a causeway heading south-east according to your micro-compass, turn to **98**.

If you wish to follow a causeway going south-west, according to your micro-compass, turn to **162**.

167

You wheel away from the Battle Fleet as the wreckage of the Eagle-Fighter plummets into the Fentusian Space Cruisers. None of the Cruisers follow you, but many of the Fentusian gunners fire shots from their laser-ports, as you escape through the ragged radar-cloak. Your tail shields are severely ruptured: deduct 2 from your defence capacity. Turn to **290**.

168

Through the Battledroid's speech translator, you ask the Flame Drake how to find Gan Tamil-Rath. After a long pause, the tiny creature looks up and says in a voice of great beauty: "Head north to the Great Metropolis of Oric, where you will find the portal to the mines. Beneath the mines you will find the Master." When he says "head north" the Flame Drake points his arm in the direction identified as south by the Battledroid's micro-compass.

You release the Flame Drake several yards away from the Lava Beast, and watch as he begins to crawl slowly towards his mount. Together they have enormous strength and intelligence. Apart, they are nothing. Turn to **218**.

169

After two kilometres, you come to a great circular iron portal, which seems to hover in mid-air. As you thrust the Battledroid forward, the portal swings open to reveal a sprawling Metropolis, previously hidden from view by an illusory force-wall. Massive towers stretch into the air, linked by twisting glass tubeways to great, glass global buildings which hover in a sky swarming with information probes.

You guide the Battledroid through the portal and into the Metropolis, along an avenue of large, loose flagstones.

If you have a Mutant Sensory Unit, turn to **89**.

If you do not, turn to **266**.

170

You realise the huge scale of the SpaceDrome as you urge the tiny Shuttle silently along the centre of the tubeway, its curved walls towering over you. After some time, you emerge unnoticed in the Droid Library, a sprawling chamber littered with viewing droids, hologram-projectors, and great shelves of data-discs.

Among the old men studying the SpaceDrome's records, you recognise the wild white mane of your Craft Master bowed over a viewing screen. You quickly thrust the Shuttle towards him. Turn to **300**.

171

The Battledroid drifts to the base of the spherical chamber, and sinks through a protoplastic air-lock, which seals off the blue liquid behind you. The compartment seems to be some sort of maintenance chamber, for the liquid has repaired minor damage to the Battledroid: roll one dice and add the score to your laser-banks up to their maximum.

The Battledroid blasts the residue of the liquid from its filters, which begin to function normally again, as you head down a vertical tubeway. Turn to **255**.

172

As the Mutant-Spore smashes to the ground, you thrust the Battledroid north along the avenue, your Rockworm guards struggling to keep pace. It is not long before the sheer glass walls and massive twisting tubeways of the SpaceDrome rise up before you.

Your guards guide you through a portal in the side of the SpaceDrome into the Holding Bay, a huge hangar, at the centre of which lies a 400-metre long Space Cruiser, suspended in the flickering light of a laser-dock. Your guards herd you into this pool of light, and as you reach the centre, the Battledroid becomes stuck fast. The Rockworms laugh cruelly up at you, before turning and departing. Turn to **50**.

173

The Battledroid's compu-speak system transmits a high-pitched squeaking laughter, which you realise is coming from the small golden-skinned creature, as it emerges from the old man's tattered robes. It stares up at you, and the computer translates its chattering voice:

"My telepathy tells me that you are sad at his death. Do not be! His time had come. I do believe you think that he was Gan Tamil-Rath. Ha, ha! You were mistaken, for I am the Droid Master you seek. He was but a Soul Server, an ancient robot who translated my voice, emotions and appearance into something you humans could understand. He was my servant and my defender, for as a Droid Master I am sworn to make no hostile action. The old Soul Server is easily replaced."

An identical old man emerges from a hidden niche, and the Droid Master leaps into the folds of his robes. "I shall speak the Droid Master's thoughts from now onwards," the Soul Server declares in your own language.

The Soul Server carries the Droid Master up into your turret and whispers, "I have been idle too long. We must pursue the Black Widow Spider Droid and save Vizo Rath, for the sake of the galaxies."

You thrust the Battledroid up the tubeway after the Spider Droid. Turn to **248**.

174

Your attack facilities have no effect on the Lava Louse. You watch in horror as it forces its shapeless body, particle by particle, into the Battledroid's control turret. Slime oozes across the screen as the Louse finally appears on the inside of your turret. It pauses, breathing heavily.

With a sudden dart, the Lava Louse flys across the control tower and hits you solidly in the chest. It bites you, then disappears. You search frantically for the strange beast, but it seems to have vanished into your body.

Feeling no ill-effect, and unable to receive any guidance from the Battledroid's computer, you resolve to press on with your quest. Note down that you have been bitten by a Lava Louse. Turn to **101**.

175

Safe from the swarming Blood Ravens, you realise how badly the red mist has burnt your skin. Deduct 2 from your life force. Heading down from the mist you see a roadway leading to a shimmering blue force-gate. To travel over the gate's rays would mean remaining in the choking mist.

*If you wish to guide the Battledroid down to the roadway in front of the force-gate, turn to **122**.*

*If you wish to thrust the Battledroid on to the roadway beyond the force-gate, deduct 2 more points from your life force and turn to **110**.*

176

The Fentusian is raising his laser sword high above his head, as he is engulfed by a dazzling cone of white light. His hideous body is instantly reduced to a residue of white powder, floating in a smoking pool of bubbling green liquid.

If you wish to await the movements of the Black Widow Spider Droid, turn to **212**.

If you wish to enter the code 231 into your Matter Transporter Pod, turn to **152**.

If you wish to attack the Spider Droid, turn to **62**.

177

A sleek black Space Trucker with a golden hawk emblazoned on its hull suddenly sweeps up towards you from Zol. Your pilot spins his couch around to face you and grins broadly, his gold tooth glinting. "I have arranged for this Trucker to carry you into the gulf, Battledroid pilot. Prepare to jettison."

He moves his gloved hand quickly across to the jettison bio-reader.

If you wish to allow the pilot to jettison you, turn to **113**.

If you have any Tali-Tokens and wish to offer them to your pilot in exchange for passage into the Fentusian Gulf, turn to **249**.

If you wish to aim the Battledroid's attack facilities at the Trucker's control turret, and order your pilot to continue into the Fentusian Gulf, turn to **83**.

178

Swarms of probes cluster about the Battledroid as you proceed along an avenue cutting through the Metropolis. They investigate curiously with probes, prods and sensors, but make no hostile action towards you.

After some two kilometres, you reach what looks like an enormous white monument. A huge marble platform hovers several metres above the ground, over a pit containing Tuskquartz crystals tumbling against each other. Above the dais hangs a thin white mist impregnated with flecks of electric-blue light.

You recognise the object as a Laser Recharger. With great relief you manoeuvre the Battledroid forward and bow its head, so that the tube above your control turret is directly over the Recharger. Inserting your hand into the Master bio-reader, you order the Battledroid to recharge.

A blinding white laser beam instantly shoots up into the Battledroid's laser-pipe. Place your laser-banks and all missile charges on maximum. Turn to **66**.

179

A three-dimensional image of Vizo Rath appears on the Battledroid's viewing-disc. He wears a high-collared scarlet robe of crushed velvet, marked with the insignia of Caluphex. His mane of white hair is brushed back from a tired, haggard face, and in his hand the Holy Emperor clasps a half-drained bottle of the potent intoxicant, Gamma-Juice. His eyes light up when he sees you, and he immediately begins babbling in a slurred, faltering voice:

"Thank Rath! You may yet be in time ... ha, ha ... I come to Oric on a mission of mercy, but Maldraggon betrays me ... ! I am besheige ... bezeige ... surrounded. Land at the northwest – er – north-east ...."

A shadow falls across Vizo Rath and his face fills with fear as you hear a croaking voice. The Holy Emperor takes a swig of

Gamma-Juice, then, with a trickle of the honeyed liquid running down his chin, he burbles timidly:

"Land on the c-c-central plains . . . er . . . there's a good chap . . . ? Oh dear!"

His radio communication suddenly ends. Turn to **286**.

180

The Drome Master suddenly darts out from a tubeway behind you and his Drome-Walker flits into one of the Battledroid's air-locks. He emerges seconds later, tumbling into your control turret. Clicking his fingers, he squeaks: "Your Space Trucker awaits you in the far reaches of the hangar. Take this money and travel well, Battledroid Master."

He throws a sack on to your control desk, scratches his head furiously while looking curiously at you from the corner of his eyes, then tumbles his Drome-Walker out of the Battledroid. Note down 200 Tali-Tokens – the currency of the galaxies – on your Items list, and turn to **100**.

181

The Standard-Investigation Probe slides slowly out from the Battledroid's chest, and into the crystal-receiver. There is a brief shower of sparks, then a massive explosion, ripping the Battledroid's control turret from its body. The tubeway is torn apart, and you plunge down into the Tuskquartz city, your life and mission at an end.

182

The viewing screen transforms itself into a radar grid, on which two blips sound. One is identified by the Battledroid's computer as a small, rapid-moving planet; the other as a large, slow-moving ship orbiting Zzyus.

*If you wish to head for the small, fast-moving planet, turn to **88**.*

*If you wish to head for the large, slow-moving ship, turn to **56**.*

183

After some 400 metres, the Battledroid emerges through a sliding portal into a massive tower. Its walls are encrusted with computer terminals, which shoot data-saturated laser-beams to each other. At the centre of the towering chamber a tiny unmanned info-shuttle darts about, centimetres above the network of laser-beam pathways.

*If you have an "x" on your Status Chart, turn to **46**.*

*If you do not, turn to **272**.*

184

You thrust the Battledroid clumsily forward, and the Rockworm falls to his knees in terror as the shadow of your craft engulfs him. There is a shower of sparks as his stun-rod clashes with your defence shields, and then you feel the Rockworm's armour buckle beneath you as he is crushed by the Battledroid's massive tracked foot. Your stomach lurches sickeningly and a cold sweat breaks from your brow as you realise the terrible thing you have done.

Looking down from the tower you see a troop of Rockworm police emerging from a portal in the centre of the roadway. Your mind muddled, you thrust the Battledroid forward into the flickering rays of the force-gate. Turn to **209**.

185

As the Battledroid thrusts forward, a bolt of forked lightning flashes its sharp fingers into the ground before you. As if in response, Oric's surface, battered by searing rain and massive fire-rocks, begins to collapse about you into a seething mass of molten lava.

If you are travelling by Hover, turn to **114**.

If you are travelling by Stride or Tracks, turn to **254**.

186

The Battledroid's flight-programme guidance systems are confused by the sweeping veils of mist, and time after time you slip away from the Alpha-2 ley-line and flounder in the fog before you find your route again. Your progress is painfully slow. Shade in five days on your Status Chart and turn to **108**.

187

You press your palm against the Independent Information Probe's flashing bio-reader, and the transparent sphere drifts silently away from the Battledroid. Your pilot couch elevates into the Probe's circular console which relays the 360° image from the Probe's infra-cams and every sound detected by its micro-bug sensors. The Probe's computer-guided remote controls fall from the console to mould into your fingers, and you thrust the probe into the tunnel.

The Probe floats along a dimly-lit tubeway which emerges in a large glass podule, at the centre of which hovers a squatly built droid. It is armed with a photon-flail of swirling laser ribbons. Through the Probe's micro-bug sensors, you hear the droid hiss rhythmically as if with breath.

Manoeuvring the Probe to the podule's ceiling, you attempt to guide it silently past the droid. Roll one dice, adding 2 to the score if your pilot skill equals 12 or more.

If the score is 4 or less, turn to 240.

If the score is 5 or more, turn to 95.

188

Showing fanatical bravery, the Rockworms thrust their Anti-Gravity Sleds through your outer defence shields, and lunge desperately with powerful teeth and claws, and hyper-charged stun-rods, at the Battledroid's exposed wiring. You must fight them as one enemy. (Range = 0)

ROCKWORM INTERGALACTIC POLICE TROOP: Attack = 9 Defence = 9 Absorption = 0 Life Reserves = 10 (Gain Bonus for Nuclear Jet) (Immune to Psi-Exuder)

If you defeat the Rockworms, turn to 40.

189

You enter a smoothly-mined tunnel illuminated by a thin yellow wire which spirals around its curved walls, giving off a hypnotic golden glow.

If you wish to head north, turn to 309.

If you wish to head south, turn to 253.

190

As you thrust the Battledroid's mighty frame into the battle, the automaton with the rotor-blade, a Fentusian Surface-Hopper, breaks free from the Flame Drake's grip. It wheels and soars away, leaving you alone to face the Flame Drake's spindly droid.

The Flame Drake outmanoeuvres you easily, and attacks from the rear from the second combat round onwards. (Range = 50m)

FLAME DRAKE'S STRIDER DROID: Attack = 14 Defence = 9 Absorption = 2 Laser Reserves = 14 (Gain Bonus for Laser Port) (Immune to Rotary Laser-Bomb Launcher)

If you defeat the Flame Drake's Strider Droid, turn to 64.

191

Your pilot engages regular bursts of light-speed as the Dragon-Class Trucker soars through the heart of Caluphex. You find your voice gradually reduced to a gravelled whisper by the high pressure of inter-planetary flight. After two days, the Trucker emerges with a shudder from a burst of light-speed travel to reveal a large green planet on its viewing screen. The pilot murmurs that he is docking to recharge his laser-banks and request computer-charts for the Fentusian Gulf. Shade in two days on your Status Chart, and turn to 297.

192

Using the probe-lever, you select the gold crystal and guide it into the crystal-receiver. The receiver melts as if touched by acid, and the portal explodes. Roll two dice and deduct the score from your laser-banks.

If the Battledroid still functions, you retrieve the gold crystal and continue through the charred remains of the portal. Turn to **315**.

193

A flickering three-dimensional image of the Space Fighter's pilot appears on your viewing-disc, his milky eyes glaring at you. The pilot's skin is transparent and through his unzipped space-suit you can see his two hearts pumping and his green veins pulsing. He is a Fentusian. An oxygen mask is perched on his long snout. As he speaks, his lizard-like tongue flicks against its clear plexoglass visor, which is clouded by his hot breath.

Your computer translates his Fentusian words:

"MD 634, Space Fighter, requesting immediate identification and clearance for landing."

If you wish to identify yourself as Battledroid SB246, turn to **121**.

If you wish to allow your computer to override, turn to **49**.

194

Urging the Battledroid on to the far side of the chamber, you engage the Automated Claw and thrust it forward. Its powerful fingers clasp the steel portal and, as you wrench the controls back, tear it from the wall. The Battledroid plunges into the tubeway, knocking the Drome Master from its path and sending his Drome-Walker ricocheting wildly between the walls of the Entrance-Bay. You engage photon-boost and flee north along the tubeway. Deduct 2 from your laser reserves and turn to **67**.

195

You open the locket and throw your head back as the dazzling radiance of the AnthraSun floods your turret. Its stunning rays shoot into the cavern and dance about its walls. The Lava Beasts rear up and cower, their eyes shutting behind the milky-skinned lids. Taking advantage of their momentary blindness, you flee.

*If you wish to power the Battledroid into the tunnel heading south from the lair of the Lava Beasts, turn to **189**.*

*If you wish to leave along the passageway going north, turn to **70**.*

196

Grabbing the Molecular Disruptor from its holster, you pick off one of the Fentusians as he bears down on you. The other Fentusian screams his deep-throated war cry and sweeps his laser sword across your skull. Roll one dice, and deduct 2 from the score if you are wearing space armour. Deduct the total from your life force.

*If you are still alive and have a mercenary with you, turn to **36**.*

*If you have no mercenary with you, turn to **111**.*

197

"Follow the Alpha-2 ley-line into the Fentusian Gulf," the figure answers. Then the cloak collapses, loose and empty, its turquoise pattern melting into a pool on the dusty floor. The metallic insects scatter, and the radio communication suddenly ends. Turn to **157**.

198

The Tuskquartz Denizen's large eyes and bleached skin are a measure of the great depth at which it lives. Pressing its arms against the tubeway's walls, it descends nimbly, leading you deeper and deeper into Oric. The tubeway soon shows signs of neglect, its walls initially being cracked, and then having fallen away from the tunnel completely.

After a descent of some ten kilometres, the Denizen scampers away through a tiny side-tunnel. You are left alone in a dusty, humid, echoing shaft, which has narrowed until the Battledroid's defence shields ignite into white flame as they brush its walls. Turn to **301**.

199

Add 2 to your pilot skill. You guide the Battledroid down on to a causeway of solidified grey lava, which emerges from a sea of molten lava, glowing crimson with blistering heat. Oric's surface is a seething mass of this searing liquid, and a heat haze dances mesmerisingly over its surface.

A short distance from you is a large platform of rock rising from the bubbling lava, and you thrust the Battledroid towards it. Turn to **77**.

200

The Flesh Mutant slithers from its shattered spore and snatches up a Hover-Bug in its gaping jaws, while you engage photon-boost and accelerate away down the steel avenue. Deduct 2 from your laser reserves.

You head north where, in the distant haze, you can make out the towering hangars of the SpaceDrome: huge laserite domes reaching over six kilometres into the sky. Turn to **47**.

201

You thrust the Battledroid through the Wolf's mouth into a steamy, dimly-lit red tunnel, and head for the pin-point of light at its far end. The light is rapidly approaching when suddenly a dark silhouette blocks it, and a large droid swoops into the tunnel. An armoury of laser cannons hangs from the droid's hull, in stark contrast to the delicate gossamer wings which flutter at its sides. Your sensors report, "Hostile Fentusian Mosquito Droid, contact 2540 milliseconds," as you engage combat mode. (Range = 500m)

FENTUSIAN MOSQUITO DROID: Attack = 14 Defence = 6 Absorption = 2 Laser Reserves = 15 (Gain Bonus for Negative-Ion Flame Thrower, Laser Port) (Immune to Nuclear Jet)

If you defeat the Mosquito Droid, you exit quickly from the tunnel: turn to 303.

202

For several minutes you stare helplessly at the Limpet Droids, sweat pouring coldly down your brow. Then they explode, blinding you for several seconds.

When you recover, you survey the severe damage to the Battledroid. Roll two dice and deduct the score from your laser-banks. Turn to 290.

203

The tunnel is beautifully cut, and its smooth walls glisten as the Battledroid's lights illuminate them. After a short distance a rougher passage branches out from the tunnel floor and sweeps back towards the surface.

If you wish to head south along the smoothly-cut tunnel, turn to 70.

If you wish to ascend the rough passageway, turn to 280.

204

The glare of its search-lights guides the Probe along the dark shaft as it pushes its way through the taut fibres of ancient cobwebs. The Probe read-out indicates that it has travelled exactly 150 metres before the ventilation shaft emerges in a large chamber. An enormous silver central viewing column is surrounded by hundreds of computers and the pumping machinery of Data Droids. You recognise the area as the SpaceDrome's Computer-Information Data Bank.

Guiding the Probe down to a large terminal, you lower its claw on to the keyboard. The claw imitates your movements, as you type into the Battledroid's computer the word: "Oric". Turn to **63**.

205

The Fentusian storm-trooper, shrieking with bloodthirsty joy, crushes you under a hail of savage blows. He continues to slash his laser sword into your body long after you have fallen. Your life and your mission end here.

206

As you activate your attack facilities, concealed laser-ports emerge from the side of the Space Trucker, confirming that it is piloted by Space Pirates. You have taken the Trucker by surprise and have first attack. Begin the combat from stage 10. (Range = 2km)

SPACE PIRATE TRUCKER: Attack = 11 Defence = 9 Absorption = 2 Laser Reserves = 14 (Gain Bonus for Laser Port)

If you win, turn to **65**.

207

You press your palm against the Mutant Sensory Unit's bio-reader, and the mutant uncoils from its socket and sways towards the computer terminals. Inserting its tongue into a computer-link, the mutant relays all the security data relating to the mines of Oric into the Battledroid's data-banks. Add 3 to your computer capacity, and write an "a" beside it. Turn to **46**.

208

After some three kilometres you come to a crossroads, its four paths stretching out across the simmering lava pools as far as you can see. From a huge blow-hole at the centre of the crossroads, a geyser suddenly throws its fountain of crystal clear water up to the level of your control turret. Steam drifts up from the great water-spout, explaining how the Hot Springs Plains got their name.

If you wish to thrust the Battledroid down through the spring's blow-hole, turn to 132.

If you wish to travel north, according to your micro-compass, turn to 275.

If you wish to head west, according to your micro-compass, turn to 77.

If you wish to head east, according to your micro-compass, turn to 48.

If you wish to head south, according to your micro-compass, turn to 105.

209

As the Battledroid plummets through the flickering rays of the force-gate, there is an explosion of blinding white light. The electric force-gate would destroy a smaller craft, but the Battledroid's defence shields absorb much of the charge. Roll one dice and deduct the score from your laser reserves.

To the accompanying hiss of its rapidly adjusting gyro-sensors, you guide the shuddering Battledroid on to the roadway beyond. Turn to 110.

210

You feel the Battledroid slow, as the unseen enemy extinguishes your hover jets and begins to engulf you. Switching the viewing screen to camera-relay, you see a translucent, formless creature, its jelly-like body filling the entire shaft. It engulfs the Battledroid's legs with its flesh, and secretes its digestive juices. Within seconds the mutant has engulfed the entire Battledroid, reducing your viewing screen's picture to a quivering slime. You must fight from inside the Water Mutant.

Fight it as normal, but deduct 2 from the Battledroid's laser-banks at the end of each combat round, as the Water Mutant deposits digestive acid on the Battledroid's armour. (Range = 0)

ORICAN WATER MUTANT: Attack = 10 Defence = 2 Absorption = 5 Laser Reserves = 30 (Gain Bonus for Negative-Ion Flame Thrower) (Immune to Laser Port)

*If you defeat the Water Mutant, turn to **91**.*

211

A hologram of the pilot appears on your viewing-disc. His most outstanding feature is simply that he has two identical heads protruding from one collar. His hair stands upright and his faces are blackened as if he had been electrocuted. A monocle is perched over one of his four squinting eyes. A pink tube droops apologetically from one of his two mouths, and runs into a huge hookah filled with a burbling blue liquid. He looks aghast at you and squawks: "Maldraggon? Why, you're not Maldraggon."

You explain your mission to this eccentric mercenary, and he replies that he has set out from Flintus-8 with the very same quest. He would be quite willing to attach his "splendid craft" to a facility holder on the Battledroid and join forces with you to conquer the evil Fentusians.

If you wish to take the mercenary along, turn to 61.

If you do not, bid him farewell and turn to 163.

212

As you watch the Black Widow Spider Droid speed away over Oric, you see a small object ejected from its hull. The Battledroid's Image Enhancer magnifies your view through the caesium-impregnated screen and you realise that the object is in fact a small man. As he plummets to the ground like some discarded puppet, you increase definition and recognise the flowing white hair and scarlet robes of Holy Emperor Vizo Rath. There is no way that you can reach him before the fatal impact, and you cradle your head in your hands as he disappears into the bubbling lava-pools of Oric. The Overseer of the Galaxy of Caluphex is dead. You have failed in your mission.

213

You press your palm gently against the facility's bio-reader, and the Mutant Sensory Unit emerges slowly from its socket. Weaving from side to side, it lowers its head to the ground, and presses its flaring nostrils against the lava. The Mutant's tongue then shoots out and flicks a piece of lava into its mouth, both for nourishment and analysis. As the Mutant Sensory Unit gradually recoils into its facility-socket once more, your computer prints up its findings: "Mutant Sensory Unit detects a fresh trail left by twenty-four mounted Lava Beasts which indicates that they headed east, according to micro-compass readings, from this point, 540,642 millisecs ago."

If you wish to use the Mutant Sensory Unit to follow the Lava Beast trail at a safe distance, turn to **18**.

If you wish to head south, according to your micro-compass, turn to **273**.

214

The tubeway emerges into a circular chamber bathed in red light, its walls lined with huge screens showing a 360° image of a great bank of rolling, swirling scarlet cloud. Inside a console at the centre of the Vapour Monitor Bay sits a programmed Robotron, a humanoid droid designed to perform repetitive functions. Glowing wires run from its empty eye-sockets up to the distant ceiling, and its ivory-white hands type rapidly and rhythmically across the blazing lights of the control desk.

If you killed a Flesh Mutant earlier in your adventure, turn to 116.

If you did not, turn to 5.

215

You unleash the Sonic Punch and the Tadpole II Neon-Security Droid, unprepared for such a primitive assault, is caught with a full-blooded blow. There is a shower of sparks and a muffled explosion. When the smoke clears, you see that the black tube now terminates in a cluster of smouldering wires. The only remains of the droid are a patch of bubbles on the surface of the pink pool.

Engaging Hover mode, you propel the Battledroid into the ornate 300-metre wide exit tubeway. Turn to 38.

216

The Rockwworm glances nervously about him, before nodding his agreement. You place the disruptor in the Matter Transporter and the weapon disappears instantly. Glancing at the viewing-disc you see the Rockworm pick it up from the control-orb hovering beside the force-gate. Remove the Molecular Disruptor from the Items listed on your Status Chart.

The Rockworm inserts his warty hand into a bio-reader, and the electric-blue portal descends. As it disappears, you thrust the Battledroid forward to the roadway beyond. Add 1 to your computer capacity. Turn to 110.

217

You feel a cool rush of oxygenated-air as the Auxiliary Oxygen Supply automatically switches in to replace the

Battledroid's spluttering filters. Life-support info-panels rise to maximum, and you start investigating this curious liquid-filled globe. It seems to be nothing more than a maintenance port for droids. There is only one exit, a tubeway at the bottom of the chamber, and correct procedure would seem to be to switch off engines and drift out through this air-locked exit. Add 2 to your computer capacity. The liquid seems to have regenerated the Battledroid: roll one dice and add the score to your laser reserves, up to their maximum.

You thrust the Battledroid through the exit tubeway. Turn to **255**.

218

Three cooled-lava causeways jut out across the molten sea from the junction upon which the towering Battledroid stands.

If you wish to go south according to your micro-compass, turn to **98**.

If you wish to go west according to your micro-compass, turn to **208**.

If you wish to go north-west according to your micro-compass, turn to **275**.

219

For two days this pilot guides you through the gulf's mists, glancing nervously over his shoulder as you scowl through the Droid-Link. Finally, he looks around and stutters: "I . . . I'm afraid this is the end of Trucker routes. I . . . I'll have to gently jettison you." Smiling pathetically, the pilot passes his palm over the jettison bio-reader, and the Battledroid drifts slowly out of the Trucker's belly and into the gulf.

Shade in two days and turn to **108**.

220

A murky image of your Craft Master forms in your mind as you clasp the Mind Choker. He looks down on you and whispers:

"Your quest nears its conclusion. The Spider Droid must be destroyed. Aim for the heart of its hull, and all will be well."

The image quickly fades and you see the Spider Droid filling your viewing screen. Following your Craft Master's advice, you lower your attack facility computer guidance systems from their alignment with the Black Widow's viewing screen, so that they lock in on the centre of the Spider Droid's hull. Add 3 to your attack capacity for the duration of the battle. Turn back to **62** and enter combat.

221

You tilt the Battledroid on to its belly and thrust it head first into the polished cargo-bay of Space Trucker Beta. It comes to rest on a cushion of laser-springs, and high-pressure hoses instantly begin cleaning down the Battledroid's hull. Your pilot glides past you along the cargo-bay's sliding footway, his cigar ablaze and his eyes twinkling. Smoothing his oily hair back, he steps into the shuttle-pod which will transport him into the Trucker's control tower. Note down that you are travelling on Space Trucker Beta and turn to **127**.

222

All attack facilities fail to respond, as you frantically wave your palm over their bio-readers. The Battledroid's computer is failing to transmit commands, as the Techno-Leach drains your data-banks. Your only option is to switch from "computer" to "manual" mode. You flick off the computer-switch, but the computer's operation light continues to glow. Even the computer is out of control! Roll one dice.

If you score 4 or less, deduct the score from your computer capacity, and roll again. If your computer capacity equals zero, the Battledroid's brain has been sucked out and your mission is over.

*If you score 5 or 6, the computer deactivates, and the manual controls and monitor screens for all facilities rise out of the control desk. Seeing your attack facilities are active again, the Flame Drake disengages the Techno-Leach and flees across the Metropolis. Turn to **318**.*

223

As the Battledroid descends into an atmosphere choked with Tuskquartz dust, a small craft appears on your viewing screen. Your computer announces: "Space Fighter – Apparent intentions: Hostile – Contact: 3010 millisecs."

If you have Gamma-Wave Intercom and wish to contact the craft, turn to **193**.

If you wish to await developments, turn to **121**.

If you wish to attack the Space Fighter, turn to **73**.

224

As the Mutant-Spore tumbles towards the Battledroid, you reactivate all attack facilities. The alarmed Rockworm Police flee through a sliding portal in the roadway, and the Hover-Bugs around you scatter wildly. You are left alone to face your enemy. Turn to **137**.

225

The Fentusian Fire-Fly has descended into the smoking mound at the centre of the cooled-lava causeway, but an enormous black robot is speeding down from the south, presumably attracted by the distress beacon. It is fully 750 metres tall and twice as long, and on its prow is a great orange painting of a globe within a flaming circle. A Fire and Ice Jet work facility hangs from the robot's side, and a huge siren blares from its roof. Its immense body covers the entire causeway, its tracks hanging over into the molten lava lake. As it senses your presence, its entire front opens into a pair of gaping jaws. It is trying to devour the Battledroid whole!

If you wish to engage photon-boost and flee north according to your micro-compass, turn to **34**.

If you wish to follow the Fentusian Fire-Fly into the smoking mound, turn to **126**.

If you wish to allow the robot to swallow you, turn to **153**.

226

The tiny Angler Droid keeps darting back towards the huge Battledroid, then flitting away again as its control-thread grows taut. It tantalisingly eludes your combat co-ordinates as you furiously pursue it down a long tubeway. The droid disappears through a wide portal, and you thrust the Battledroid through in pursuit.

You enter a massive foul-smelling cavern, stalactites jutting down from its ceiling. At the centre of the chamber stands a 400-metre tall Robo-Mutant, bobbing the Angler Droid from its hand like a yo-yo. The Robo-Mutant's hideous reptilian body ends in a long swishing tail, while its head is made up of a slimy green skull interlocked with panels of intricate droid machinery. One of its eyes is a red speck at the centre of a steel orb, while the other flickers wetly with life. The Robo-

Mutant grins, snarls, then launches into a frenzied attack. (Range = 250m)

ROBO-MUTANT AND ANGLER DROID: Attack = 15 Defence = 7 Absorption = 4 Laser Reserves = 14 (Gain Bonus for Laser Port) (Immune to Sonic Punch)

If you defeat the Robo-Mutant, there is an exit tunnel heading north. Turn to **8**.

227

You programme instructions into the Automated Claw's personal computer, and the great metal arm reaches slowly up to the Limpet Droids. Roll one dice, and add 2 if your computer capacity is 10 or more.

If the score is 4 or more, the Limpet Droid is removed successfully by the Automated Claw.

If the score is 3 or less, the Limpet Droid detonates. Roll one dice and deduct the score from your laser-banks.

Repeat the process for the second Limpet Droid, then turn to **290**.

228

The tubeway emerges in a huge, low-ceilinged gallery, poorly illuminated by thousands of hovering lumo-globes. You can feel the massive weight of rock above you bearing down oppressively. An assortment of eccentrically designed droids stand idly in massive glass pods, and several glass display cases hold the grotesque, mummified remains of small men, their swollen skulls tattooed with the orb and blazing ring symbol of the Droid Masters.

In the centre of the gallery hovers a heavy, round marble platform. A thin white mist impregnated with flecks of electric-blue light, swirls above the platform, while below it clusters of Turkquartz crystals tumble against each other. The apparatus is a Laser Charger, and pressing your palm against the Master bio-reader, you instruct the Battledroid to recharge.

Place your laser-banks and missile charges on maximum, and turn to **55**.

229

The Drome Master thrusts a hand through the skin of his Drome-Walker and snatches up the Travel Crystal. Juggling it heavily from hand to hand, he examines it, then looks at you with a broad smile. "Follow the tubeway north to the Docking Hangar," he pipes shrilly. "I will arrange your passage." He guides his Drome-Walker out of the turret, pausing only to shoot out a large silver bubble which floats up and rests against the Battledroid's viewing screen. (Make a note of this on your Status Chart.)

As he leaves the Entrance Bay through a tiny portal, you thrust the Battledroid through the exit tubeway. Turn to **67**.

230

The portal slides open and, as you guide the Battledroid along a new tubeway, your computer announces: "We are now at the very heart of Oric."

You thrust the Battledroid through the end of the tubeway into a magnificent subterranean laboratory. Half-completed droids hover in mid-air above dancing streams of coloured gas, or rest in the white rubber grips of sparking machines. Tuskquartz crystals tumble in a great glass vat beside you, shooting laser beams eccentrically about the laboratory, to ignite the churning engines that line its walls.

In the centre of the chamber, a small man lies back in the palm of a huge, white metallic hand, which floats several metres above the ground. He wears a flowing green robe patterned with darting flecks of bright light, its fine grey fringe standing upright as if charged with static electricity. The old man's skull is swollen at the top and blue veins throb in his temples. His forehead is tattooed with the orb and fiery circle design of the Droid Masters. A tiny, wide-eyed, golden-skinned creature with a flowing lion's-mane and long delicate claws nestles in the folds of his robe, staring curiously at the Battledroid.

The old man glances up at you, and lazily snaps his fingers, which are bejewelled with ornate silver rings. A small, sleek, golden droid instantly swoops from the chamber's rocky ceiling and glides elegantly towards you. It releases a billowing pink gas which engulfs you. The Battledroid begins to rise uncontrollably into the air, towards the soothing grey light of a strange portal which hovers above you.

If you wish to fire your attack facilities up into the air, turn to 72.

If you wish to fire your attack facilities down against the chamber's floor, turn to 161.

231

The corridor widens into a large tubeway, its walls punctuated with white discs from which shoot intermittent pulses of electricity. The tubeway begins to spiral upwards, eventually ending in a round portal. Beside it is an illuminated pad with which to open the sliding door. Above you rises a ventilation shaft.

If you wish to guide the Shuttle up the ventilation shaft, turn to 257.

If you wish to open the sliding portal by touching the pressure pad with the Shuttle's grab, turn to 107.

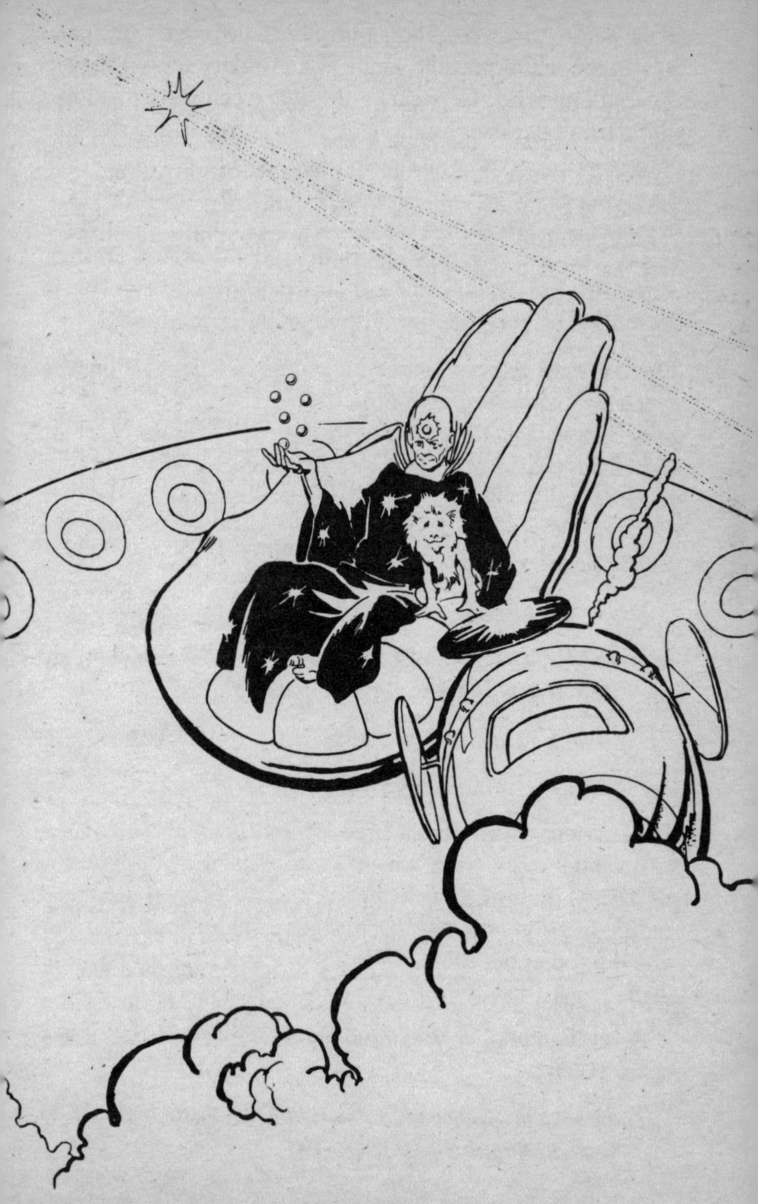

232

You touch the Shuttle's glowing red info-panel and your contoured Pilot Couch instantly descends through the floor of the control turret. There is a hiss as a compressed-air lift carries you down through the Battledroid, until you emerge behind the Shuttle's controls. You roll the palm of your hand over the control sphere, and the Shuttle gently disengages from the Battledroid. Turn to **170**.

233

The Automated Claw shoots out and snatches the Flame Drake from his turret. The effect on the Lava Beast is instantaneous, and astonishing. The enormous creature ceases to breathe fire and staggers about as if blinded, its head tossing in anguish. The Lava Beast collides with the Battledroid's legs, then falls to its knees at the Battledroid's feet.

The Flame Drake screams and kicks at the Automated Claw, but it is held fast. It looks down at its fallen mount, then glances up at you, tears welling in its large eyes.

*If you wish to question the Flame Drake, turn to **168**.*

*If you do not, turn to **218**.*

234

The tubeway is blocked, midway over the Droid Master's subterranean Tuskquartz city, by a large portal. It is carved from Tuskquartz-ore, and crackles with an unleashed energy that manifests itself in streaks of dancing blue light. At the centre of the portal is carved the number 50, and below it is a crystal-receiver.

*If you have a crystal with a diamond at its centre and wish to insert it, turn to **19**.*

If you have a crystal with a gold coin at its centre and wish to insert it, turn to **80**.

If you have a crystal with a silver coin at its centre and wish to insert it, turn to **124**.

If you have none of these crystals, or wish to insert the Battledroid's Standard-Investigation Probe into the crystal-receiver, turn to **181**.

235

You urge the Battledroid through the converging Rockworm ranks, along the blazing roadway of light, and into the breathtaking expanse of the Hangar. The light-bridge has retracted half-way, leaving a 50-metre wide void over a shimmering blue pool of laser-beams.

If you are travelling by Stride, turn to **7**.

If you are travelling by Tracks, turn to **106**.

If you are travelling by Hover, turn to **311**.

236

If you selected a Psi-Exuder as your attack facility, turn to **139**.

If you selected any other attack facility, turn to **174**.

237

The picture that pieces itself together before your eyes is not a pretty one. At the centre of a dank cave, a bloated Robo-Mutant sits back on its haunches, scratching its smooth green belly, and dribbling. Its two gangling clawed legs, its powerful arms and its twisted horned face, with a gnarled, protruding snout, are all typical of a mutant. Its chest, though, is constructed from laserite rods and discs, pumping pistons, and throbbing laser-banks, where this foul creature has been the subject of some demented droid-professor's experiments. The Robo-Mutant's red-eyed gaze informs you that it is not best pleased with your sudden materialisation at the centre of its sanctuary.

In its deformed right claw, the Robo-Mutant clasps a 30-metre long laser whip, the tips of its long tongues highly charged with laser bolts.

If you wish to attack the Robo-Mutant's right side, turn to **289**.

If you wish to attack the Robo-Mutant's left side, turn to **138**.

238

As you emerge from the cargo-bay, a dust-covered droid staggers up to you and offers to recharge the Battledroid's laser-banks, gesturing stiffly at the lumbering Mobile-Recharger behind him. This is a standard extra when a Space Trucker is being recharged. You thank him and show him into the cargo-bay.

Pushing through the crowds you are suddenly halted by a tug at your sleeve. A tiny bald-headed man, floating at your side on a shimmering silver levi-disc, shouts up at you: "Space armour! Space armour! Only 100 Tali-Tokens to be guarded from pirates, marauders and the evil Fentusians!" A four metre tall albino mutant, his colourless head thrust down deep between his powerful shoulders, strides forward and dangles a battered suit of space armour before you, holding it delicately between two fingers. If you have 100 Tali-Tokens and wish to add space armour to your Items list, adjust your Status Chart accordingly. Turn to **21**.

239

You attack the Fentusian Surface-Hopper with the help of the Flame Drake's droid. At Stage 1 of each combat round, roll one dice. If the score is 1–3, the Surface-Hopper attacks you as normal. If the score is 4–6, the Surface-Hopper attacks the Flame Drake: go straight to stage 10. At the end of each combat round, deduct 3 points from the Surface-Hopper's laser reserves to represent the damage inflicted by the Flame Drake. (Range = 50m)

FENTUSIAN SURFACE-HOPPER: Attack = 14 Defence = 8 Absorption = 2 Laser Reserves = 13 (Gain bonus for Negative-Ion Flame Thrower) (Immune to Psi-Exuder)

If you defeat the Fentusian Space-Hopper, turn to **166**.

240

The picture on the probe-monitor suddenly disappears, and is reduced to a mass of static interference. No signal returns from the Information Probe, and it fails to respond to your computer signals. The Probe is lost, and you are left to ponder on what method the droid used to detect and destroy it. Cross off the Independent Information Probe from your list of facilities, remove it from Figure 2 and deduct its weight from the Battledroid's total weight.

If you have a Manually-Operated Shuttle, you may pilot it into the stone-claw entrance to your left: Turn to 293.

Alternatively, you may guide the Battledroid into the main hallway through the Stone Wolf's jaws: Turn to 201.

241

As you pass your hand over the Intercom bio-reader, a flickering 3-dimensional hologram of the Aero-Limo pilot appears on the circular viewing-disc at the centre of the Battledroid's control turret. He is particularly ugly, even for a Rockworm, and yellowed teeth show beneath his rubbery green lips as he snarls, "What is your Security Clearance Number?"

If you wish to give him a false Security Clearance Number, turn to 59.

If you would prefer to make a polite request for a Travel Crystal, the travel permit held by all the Rockworms and government officials, turn to 24.

If you have a Missile Attack Facility and wish to fire a warning shot across the Aero-Limo's bows, demanding that the Rockworm send you a Travel Crystal, turn to 160.

242

A brooding storm begins to stir itself up as you strike out across the plateau. The sky turns a deep purple, and dark clouds rumble ominously towards you. Streaks of forked lightning illuminate Oric's surface, and tiny chunks of scorching lava begin to hail down against the Battledroid's turret. They soon grow into great fire-rocks which flame furiously as they hammer against your defence shields.

If you wish to engage photon-boost, and rush into the heart of the fire-storm, deduct 2 from your laser reserves and turn to **185**.

If you wish to await the fire-storm's passing, turn to **26**.

243

The Crevasse Crawler flicks its thin tail around the Battledroid's feet and entwines itself around the Battledroid, its slick body seeming to thrill at the glowing touch of your defence shields. The Battledroid is thrown off balance and plunges down into the crevasse, with the Crevasse Crawler coiled about it.

You continue to battle against the twisting, slithering creature as you plummet down and down, for what seems like an eternity.

Roll two dice and add your pilot skill to the score.

If the total is 15 or less, turn to **148**.

If the total is 16 or more, turn to **41**.

244

For two days the Trucker soars on through Caluphex. It slows to sub-light-speed to sweep between the jet black twin stars of Platinus, and again to orbit the ice-encrusted surface of the barren planet Jethal. Here, the Battledroid intercepts a weak radio transmission, translating only the Fentusian words "*serazith*" meaning "go", and "*gazith*" meaning "stop", before the signal fades.

Then the trucker locks into light-speed co-ordinates for the last time to carry you to the limits of the Caluphex Reaches. Shade in two days on your Status Chart, and turn to **96**.

245

You pass your palm over the Oxygen Supply's bio-reader, and a rush of cool, highly-oxygenated air gusts into the control turret. You engage Stride movement, and the Battledroid swims about the underground lake, searching for an exit. You find a tunnel descending from the bottom of the lake directly below the blow-hole. Water is kept from the exit tunnel by air-pressure, created by the hot steam which is building up as the geyser prepares to blow again.

You thrust the Battledroid quickly down the tunnel. Turn to **126**.

246

The molten lava beside the junction suddenly erupts, and the Battledroid hisses under a shower of scorching liquid. An immense creature leaps from the lava lake. Its eyes burn red with fury, and flames lick the spikes on its back. A tiny creature urges the beast on from a turret on the back of its neck. Your computer screams: "Flame Drake mounted on Lava Beast!" and the massive creature leaps at the Battledroid, its jaws spitting flames. (Range = 200m) The Lava Beast attacks from the rear.

LAVA BEAST AND FLAME DRAKE: Attack = 15 Defence = 3 Absorption = 3 Laser Reserves = 15 (Gain bonus for Laser Port, Psi-Exuder) (Immune to Negative-Ion Flame Thrower)

*If you have an Automated Claw and wish to use it at stage 10 of a combat round instead of attacking, turn to **97**.*

*If you defeat the Lava Beast and Flame Drake, turn to **9**.*

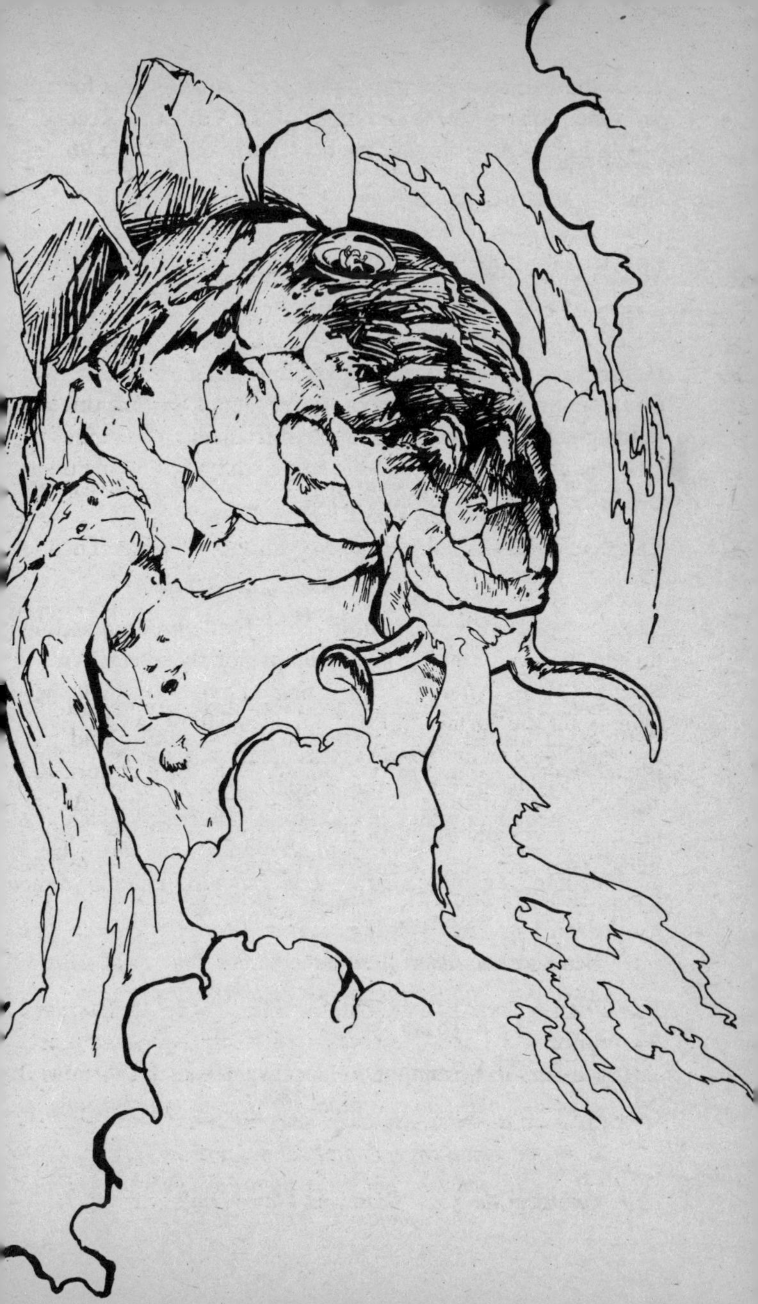

247

You feel a burning pain in your chest and a sensation as if something is squirming inside your body. Suddenly, a Lava Louse bursts from your chest, hauling its writhing body between your ribs. The hideous creature falls to the floor and slithers out through the Battledroid's viewing screen, as you collapse in agony. Roll one dice, add 2 to the score, and deduct the total from your life force.

If you are still alive, you lie still while the Battledroid's control-turret medical-probes hover about you, frantically binding your chest and injecting pain-killers.

Hauling yourself back into your pilot's couch, you doggedly continue your quest. Turn back to **68**.

248

Engaging photon-boost, you drive the Battledroid on and on up the tubeway, waiting for a glimpse of the Black Widow Spider Droid. After an exhausting climb, you finally re-emerge on the surface of Oric. On a radiant dais floating in the middle of a molten-lava sea stands a great grey stone building, constructed in the shape of an enormous wolf. There is a small entrance in each of its clawed feet, while the only passageway large enough to accomodate the Battledroid ascends into its gaping, sharp-toothed mouth. The top of the Wolf Tower is shrouded in a heavy mist.

If you have an Independent Information Probe and wish to dispatch it into the tiny tunnel under the stone claw to your right, turn to **187**.

If you have a Manually-Operated Shuttle and wish to pilot it into the small tunnel beneath the claw to your left, turn to **293**.

Alternatively, you may guide the Battledroid into the entrance through the wolf's mouth by turning to **201**.

249

The pilot nods his agreement, and you despatch all your Tali-Tokens to him through the Battledroid's Matter Transporter. Remove them from your Status Chart.

He collects the tokens, slicks back his hair with a stroke of his hand, and hisses: "Thank you for your gift, Battledroid Master!" To your horror, he reaches quickly over to the jettison bio-reader. Turn to **113**.

250

With one blast of a Battledroid attack facility, the robotron explodes, showering you with burning debris, and briefly illuminating the steel cavern. Leaving the droid's charred remains behind, you thrust the Battledroid into a tunnel which heads south and descends into Oric's heart. Turn to **203**.

251

As you launch into combat mode, the automated gun-ship wheels and races back to meet your attack. It moves at such high speed that it is very difficult to hit. For the first combat round and every odd round, the range is three kilometres. For the second round, and every even round, it has closed the range to 250 metres. Select your attack facilities for each round accordingly. (Range = 250m/3km)

FENTUSIAN AUTOMATED GUN-SHIP: Attack = 13 Defence = 12 Absorption = 2 Laser Banks = 10 (Gain Bonus for Heat Seeking Atomic Torpedo Launcher, Sonic Punch) (Immune to Nuclear Jet)

If you defeat the Fentusian Automated Gun-Ship, turn to **299**.

252

The tubeway emerges into the Security Bay, a hexagonal chamber flooded in a dim blue light. A pathway of dazzling yellow light stretches from the tubeway's mouth to the other side of the room where it extends into a 100 metre-wide light-bridge, reaching out into the vast expanse of the Drome's Docking Hangar.

The Security Bay is filled with the skulking, shadowed figures of Rockworm Security Police, lurking in Space-Sleds, Hover-Pods and on foot, at the side of the light-path.

If your control-turret is marked by a Drome Master's golden or silver bubble, turn to **125**.

If it is not, turn to **37**.

253

The tunnel emerges in a large circular chamber, its smooth walls glistening beneath a wet coat of slime. The smooth floor of the chamber slopes into the mouth of a vertical shaft at its centre, and the Battledroid has to scrabble to avoid sliding down into the tunnel. A second tunnel exits to the north.

At the centre of the chamber hang the lifeless bodies of a Fentusian stormtrooper and a Rockworm security guard. They are gruesomely cocooned in sticky grey webs, and dangle by thin threads from the ceiling. You are not sure if their bodies are cocooned to preserve them or as some primitive ritualistic warning to intruders.

If you wish to select Hover mode, and guide the Battledroid down the vertical shaft, turn to **78**.

If you wish to direct the Battledroid into the tunnel heading north, turn to **189**.

254

The Battledroid tumbles into a gaping crater, crashing down amongst the fire-rocks and slithering into a pool of molten lava. Roll one dice and deduct the score from your laser-reserves. Glancing about the crater, you see the mouth of a tunnel descending into the heart of the planet. It is your only hope of sanctuary from the ferocious fire-storm. Turn to **126**.

255

You continue along the tubeway for a short while before coming to a marbled white portal, which swings silently open as you approach. You thrust the Battledroid through it and head along a ribbed tubeway, heading east for some time, before your Image Enhancer relays a picture of two humanoid creatures in the tunnel ahead. The computer identifies them as Tuskquartz Denizens.

They are extremly thin and sinewy, and their skin is a very pale white. Their backs are bent so that their boned claws lie lamely on the ground, while their legs are splayed apart behind them. The creatures' long skulls are dominated by enormous, dilated eyes and wide, flaring nostrils, while a long forked tongue lolls from their snouts. The smaller of the two creatures has the largest, most haunting eyes, and his skin is far more bleached. They sense the Battledroid, and scurry off down the separate tubeways.

If you wish to follow the larger Tuskquartz Denizen, turn to **53**.

If you wish to follow the smaller, paler Tuskquartz Denizen, turn to **198**.

256

"I smell death upon you," the Drome Master declares, his squeaking voice echoing through the Entrance Bay. "Deactivate your droid!"

The piercing whistle of an alert siren suddenly fills the SpaceDrome, and three troops of Rockworm police charge out from tubeways in the floor of the chamber. The Drome Master flits rapidly to the far side of the Entrance Bay, where the only large exit portal starts to slide slowly shut.

If you have an Automated Claw and wish to activate it, turn to **194**.

If you do not have this facility, or do not wish to use it, turn to **90**.

257

Climbing the shaft, you finally emerge in a tapering glass spire, over a transparent ledge filled with a dense silver liquid.

Below you a cluster of clear-skinned Fentusians, clad in heavy black space armour, are beginning the ascent of a "ladder of light". This dazzling anti-gravity cone leads up to the hulking Black Widow Spider Droid which lurks in the mists outside of the building. It balances precariously on the transparent spire, its jointed metallic legs clinging to the glass wall only centimetres from the Shuttle's screen. You thrust the Shuttle into the shadows as the Fentusian stormtroopers ascend into the darkness of the Spider Droid. You recognise the last of them as the evil Fentusian Death General Violwart. Turn to **84**.

258

Following the Central Hot Springs Plains co-ordinates, you plunge into Oric's atmosphere. It is choked with white Tuskquartz dust, which clings to your viewing screen as fast as the Battledroid's hydro-wipers can blast it away.

There is a sudden shower of sparks and the Battledroid is sent reeling as it clashes against two fluorescent laser rails. You fight desperately to control the shuddering Battledroid, regretting ruefully the days of your apprenticeship spent idling among the museum exhibits instead of training on the Flight Simulation computer. Roll one dice and add the score to your pilot skill. Add 2 if you have Satellite-Informed Radar Scan.

*If your score is 11 or less, turn to **42**.*

*If your score is 12 or more, turn to **123**.*

259

After some 500 metres, you halt the mighty Battledroid at a junction. A rough-hewn passageway leads off to the east, its rugged walls running with a sticky blue luminous fluid. The craggy passageway runs for several metres before joining a laser bridge of sheer red light. This in turn heads to a round compartment. Its roof and floor are lined with jagged white crystals, between which shoot the mesmerising rays of flourescent blue laser beams.

If you wish to head north, along the glass tubeway, turn to 264.

If you wish to travel south along the glass tubeway, turn to 183.

If you wish to travel through the rugged passageway and cross the light-bridge into the chamber, turn to 13.

260

The control turret is choked with blood-red fumes, and you feel consciousness slipping away from you. The foul creatures batter their fractured leathery wings against the glass only metres from your stinging eyes, as the Battledroid's controls slip from your grasp. As the Battledroid plummets down through the sickly vapour, you hear a Blood Raven clattering towards you along some hidden air-channel, before you black out. Turn to 12.

261

The hum of your laser banks is silenced, and the Battledroid stands lifeless and defenceless as the heat-seeking missile flys on towards you. You shut your eyes, and prepare for the impact, as it looms larger and larger on your screen. . . .

At the last moment the heat-seeking missile veers off course and plummets harmlessly into the crimson sea. The heat of the molten lava is greater than that of the deactivated Battledroid, and the missile's sensors were fooled.

Add 2 to your computer capacity and turn to 225.

262

The old man beats his palm with his fist as the diamond-crystal appears before him. Then he cranes his neck to look up to your turret. Your Image Enhancer reveals a thin smile playing on his lips as he whispers: "I will help your quest with all haste. The Battledroid is in great need of adjustment."

You shut down the Battledroid as the old man steps on to a levy-disc and darts up to begin work on his old creation's internal circuitry. An info-probe hovers beside his ear, whispering advice and shooting out thin grabs to snatch the laser-tools that float about the laboratory's ceiling. The golden-skinned creature scampers up and down the old man's robe, using its delicate claws to attach wires and new components.

Suddenly, there is a shattering explosion from behind you, and a massive, sleek black Fentusian Spider Droid swoops into the laboratory, its laser-ports blazing. The Battledroid's wiring is incomplete and it stands defenceless.

If you wish to reactivate the Battledroid, turn to 143.

If you wish to wait for the old man to finish rewiring the Battledroid, turn to 30.

263

The massive explosions of your fierce combat have cleared the great steel avenue for several hundred metres about the Battledroid. To the north, you can just see through the heat haze the huge six kilometre high domed hangars of the SpaceDrome. Selecting a movement mode, you head towards them. Turn to 47.

264

The passage emerges into a breath-taking cavern, traversed by a narrow causeway just wide enough for the Battledroid's tracked feet. Either side of the Battledroid is a huge drop into a dark crevasse, its distant floor lined with a grey, moss-choked webbing. Leathery fronds hang down from the cavern roof high above you. You guide the Battledroid gingerly across the crevasse, until it comes to rest on a large, circular silver platform at the centre of the cavern. Turn to **150**.

265

Another Space Trucker suddenly sweeps up towards you from Zol, a huge golden hawk symbol emblazoned on its side. Your pilot speaks briefly through his intercom, then turns to you, a look of concern on his face, and says: "This craft's pilot says he wishes to carry you into the gulf. If you would prefer to stay on my Trucker, I will outrun him and transport you closer to Oric for two hundred Tali-Tokens."

*If you have two hundred Tali-Tokens and wish to remain on Dragon-Class Alpha, deduct the tokens from your Status Chart and turn to **79**.*

*If you do not have the money, or do not wish to spend it, turn to **113**.*

266

As the Battledroid proceeds along the broad avenue, heading west according to micro-compass readings, hundreds of tiny probes flit about your turret like insects, their electronic eyes flicking as they collect data.

*If you are travelling by Hover or Stride, turn to **141**.*

*If you are travelling by Tracks, turn to **318**.*

267

The pilot nods his agreement, and begins programming the flight control computer positioned above his right shoulder, announcing, "Prepare for light-speed engagement."

The SpaceDrome's Docking-Portals slide slowly apart and the Trucker pilot thrusts his craft's control column violently forward. The Trucker trembles and shudders as its great engines roar. Suddenly, the skin on your face draws tight. There is a loud bang, and you seem to be flying through a tunnel of streaming colours. The colours merge into a tunnel of bright light, and you are travelling at light-speed through the galaxy. Turn to **119**.

268

You draw the Molecular Disruptor from its holster but it tumbles from the sweating palm of your trembling hand. As you scrabble across the floor to reclaim it, the Fentusian leaps with great agility across the control turret. Screaming his war-cry, he slashes his laser-sword through you. Roll one dice and deduct 2 from the score if wearing space armour. Deduct the total from your life force.

If you still live, you grasp the Molecular Disruptor and thrust it at the Fentusian as he leaps towards you. Turn to **176**.

269

A fleet of small communication probes suddenly sweep past the Battledroid, their aerials glowing as they transmit coded messages. Your computer intercepts the signal and prints out a message on your viewing screen, while explaining that it is translated from Fentusian.

"Fire-Fly Droid positioned on Central Hot Springs Plains. Strider Robot erected."

Add 2 to your computer capacity, and turn to **290**.

270

The digi-ring disappears from your finger as you turn it to the left, and the Fentusians stand before you completely unharmed. (Remove the digi-ring from your Status Chart).

The Fentusians lunge forward, and you feel the blows from their laser swords cutting into you. Roll two dice and deduct 4 from the score if you are wearing space armour. Deduct the total from your life force.

If you are still alive and have a mercenary with you, turn to 36.

If you are still alive and have no mercenary, but have a Molecular Disruptor, turn to 196.

If you do not have a mercenary or Molecular Disruptor with you, turn to 205.

271

Alarmed pilots swing their Hover-Bugs away from you, as the Battledroid plants its huge tracks upon the granite roadway at the centre of a large crossroads. The path north, heading directly to the SpaceDrome, is blocked several hundred metres ahead by a flickering blue force-gate and its Rockworm sentry. An Aero-Limo, a sleek black shuttle carrying some dignitary or official, sweeps along the eastern pass which disappears into the peaks. To the west, a lumbering Securi-Pod, a plate-armoured grey globe carrying members of the Intergalactic police, drifts along only centimetres above the surface of a similar pass. You must select a terranean movement mode – Hover, Stride or Tracks – and choose which path to follow:

If you wish to head north, turn to 81.

If you wish to head east, turn to 165.

If you wish to head west, turn to 43.

272

Place an "x" on your Status Chart.

The computer screens suddenly print up images of various angles of the Battledroid, and you realise that you are being monitored. From the far side of the tower, a security automaton lumbers towards you, its massive limbs heavily shielded by laserite armour. While similar in size to the Battledroid, it has no control turret, its neck terminating in a ribbed tube stretching to the chamber's distant roof.

Your sensors indicate that the headless automaton is armed for close combat. As the attack-monitors rise up from your control panel, the automaton grasps the Battledroid with a giant pincer and swings an 80-metre laser sword which slices, shimmering, through the air towards your control turret.

Sparks shower from the two towering droids as they lock together in ferocious gladiatorial combat.

The Battledroid's computer announces that Sonic Punch and Negative-Ion Flame Thrower can be used simultaneously against this opponent. (Range = 0)

> *If you wish to attack the computer terminals instead of the Gladiator Droid at stage 10 of any combat round, deduct 2 from your laser-banks and turn to* **146**.

> DROID MASTER'S GLADIATOR: Attack = 13 Defence = 8 Absorption = 2 Laser Reserves = 15 (Gain Bonus for Negative-Ion Flame Thrower, Sonic Punch: combine bonus if you have both) (Immune to Psi-Exuder.)

If you win and have a Mutant Sensory Unit, turn to **207**.

If you win but do not have this facility, turn to **46**.

273

After two kilometres an enormous circular iron portal blocks the causeway, hovering in mid-air with flames licking at its sides. As you thrust the Battledroid forward the portal slides open, revealing a sprawling Metropolis which was previously shrouded from view by an illusion-generating force-wall. Whole towns hover among the clouds above the Metropolis, linked to towering crystal skyscrapers on the ground by sweeping laser-rails and twisting glass tubeways. The whole city swarms with unmanned satellites and probes. You eagerly urge the Battledroid through the portal and into the Metropolis. Turn to **109**.

274

The Trucker speeds through the vast Caluphex Galaxy, slowing to a sub-light speed at regular intervals to negotiate asteroid storms. After two days of space travel you feel weak and dizzy from space sickness, despite the regular handfuls of bitter zincite capsules you have wearily swallowed. Your head aches as the Trucker slows, the scream of its engines descending to a throbbing drone, and you emerge from the blinding tunnel of light speed once more.

Shade in two days on your Status Chart, and turn to **85**.

275

If you are travelling by Hover, deduct 2 from your laser banks. You travel for some three kilometres, before coming to a crossroads. Turn to **299**.

276

The Battledroid crashes up against the domed roof of the chamber, only the mercury-gas shock absorbers in the pilot's couch preventing you from being flung through the viewing screen. The blue liquid is now seeping into the turret through seals damaged by the impact. The lighting flickers, threatening to plunge you into darkness, and your life-support monitor plummets towards zero.

If you wish to allow the Battledroid to sink down to the bottom of the globe, turn to **171**.

If you wish to propel the Battledroid to the far side of the chamber, turn to **312**.

277

The shimmering blue force-gate descends rapidly to the ground, and the Rockworm guard lumbers aside, eyeing you suspiciously. Selecting a movement mode, you thrust the Battledroid forward along the roadway and, as you pass the

Rockworm, the force-gate springs back up behind you. Turn to **110**.

278

The tubeway is blocked by a second portal, identical to the first but for the fact that it has the number 60 inscribed upon it.

*If you wish to insert the crystal with a diamond at its centre, turn to **158**.*

*If you wish to insert the crystal with a gold coin at its centre, turn to **39**.*

*If you wish to insert the crystal with a silver coin at its centre, turn to **58**.*

*If you wish to insert the Battledroid's Standard Investigation Probe into the crystal-receiver, turn to **181**.*

279

For days you guide the Battledroid through the Fentusian Gulf, which seems empty and endless. The mists swirl about the Battledroid, rocking it continuously, and confusing your senses.

*If you have Satellite-Informed Radar Scan, turn to **140**.*

*If you do not, turn to **186**.*

280

Deduct 2 from your laser-banks if travelling by Hover. After several hundred metres, the tunnel swings around and begins to descend once more. As it sweeps south again, an even rougher passageway, its mouth edge hung with trailing cobwebs, breaks away and ascends northward.

If you wish to continue south, turn to **136**.

If you wish to thrust the Battledroid through the mouth of the northward passageway, turn to **86**.

281

You pass your palm over the Gamma-Wave Intercom bio-reader, and a shimmering 3-dimensional image appears on the Battledroid's viewing-disc. It shows a plump figure shrouded in a loose cloak of swirling turquoise and green patterns, his face veiled in the shadows of a large hood. The strange apparition hovers several metres above the floor of a dusty cave and a dozen large four-winged metallic insects flutter around it, through the strands of an enormous white cobweb. The cloaked figure speaks softly to you: "Ironis-2 is abandoned, my friend. The all-wise Droid Masters flee the foolishness of Voril Rath's acid words. What would you know of them?"

If you wish to ask the quickest route to Oric, turn to **197**.

If you wish to ask the whereabouts of the last Droid Master, Gan Tamil-Rath, turn to **27**.

If you wish to end the communication, turn to **157**.

282

The Scout-Wasp plummets down through Oric's atmosphere, which is choked by clouds of Tuskquartz dust. It glides between the great laser-rails which stretch from Oric to the marbled face of Zzyus, looming ominously in the distance.

You emerge over a fiery landscape, grey cooled-lava causeways jutting out across seething seas of crimson molten lava. The Scout-Wasp lands gracefully on a crossroads, still clutching the Battledroid in its massive claws, like some great hawk with its prey. Its trailing yellow wires sink into the pools of boiling lava, and its four leathery wings continue to beat softly.

Two Fentusians emerge from the Scout-Wasp's control tower, clutching flickering laser swords. Striding into the foot of the Battledroid, they begin their ascent to your turret. Turn to **131**.

283

You pass your hand over the bio-reader, and the Automated Claw glides swiftly out from its socket. Holding the astonished robotron still with two large, steel fingers, it plucks the Tuskquartz Globe gently from its back, and plugs it into a vacant facility socket on the Battledroid. Its blue anti-gravity jets form a haze beneath the new facility. Your info-panels inform you that the facility is locked in, and registers its weight as zero. Note the Tuskquartz Globe on your Status Chart. This facility has 3 charges, each restoring one dice of laser points. You may use 1 charge at the END of any encounter.) Add 1 to your computer capacity.

You exit through the north tubeway, thrusting the Battledroid past the indignant robotron which is shaking its head furiously, shouting: "Why! That's outrageous... give that back at once, you lumbering lump of iron... I say...!" Turn to **8**.

284

The Drome Master suddenly darts out from a tubeway and flits up to the Battledroid. He shoots into one of the Battledroid's air-locks and seconds later his Drome-Walker tumbles into your control turret. He giggles shrilly, rubs his eyes with the knuckles of one spindly hand, then pipes: "Your Space Trucker awaits you on the far side of the Hangar, Battledroid Master. Please take these gifts and hold your head high against Maldraggon."

He thrusts a leather sack jingling with Tali-Tokens – the currency of the galaxies – and a heavy black ring on to your control desk. "Twist the digi-ring to the right if a creature disputes ownership of your control turret," the Drome Master says with a mischievous grin. "I wish you well." Stroking his nose in an ancient Caluphexian salute, the Drome Master departs, somersaulting his bobbing Drome-Walker through an air-lock and into the Docking Hangar.

Note 300 Tali-Tokens and a digi-ring on your Items list, and turn to **100**.

285

The defeated Spider Droid shatters into fragments, but from its shell emerges a sleeker, darker craft. It swoops past the Battledroid and unleashes a laser shot which blasts the old man from his levy-disc, before fleeing through a tubeway in the roof of the laboratory.

The old man lies burnt and lifeless on the floor of the chamber. Without the help of the Droid Master, your quest is doomed . . . Turn to **173**.

286

The Holy Emperor Vizo Rath is Independent Overseer of the entire Caluphex Galaxy, and sole heir to the Rath Dynasty. His voice-pattern and palm-print hold the key to all Security Portals and Space Gates of the surrounding galaxies. His capture by Maldraggon would seal your galaxy's fate, and the rescue of Vizo Rath now becomes a vital part of your quest. The Battledroid's sensory-scan locks into his life-force, selecting it in seconds from the millions of life-forms in the galaxy. It duplicates the thud of his heartbeat on your audio transmitter, as a nagging reminder of his peril, so that you will know instantly if his life is taken.

The Battledroid prints up three possible landing areas on the tiny volcanic surface of Oric.

If you wish to land on the central Hot Spring Plains, turn to **258**.

If you wish to land on the north-east Hot Spring Plains, turn to **69**.

If you wish to land on the north-west Hot Spring Plains, turn to **144**.

287

As the Flame Drake appears on your viewing-disc, his wide, sorrowful eyes narrow and he snarls at you. Upon seeing the Droid Master's Symbol, though, his eyes widen, and he looks at you with a broad, grey-toothed smile. You ask him how to find Gan Tamil-Rath, and he replies:

"Well, personally, I fly east to the golden gates of Oric's Metropolis, then north to the bronze portal, where I seek the deepest, darkest tunnel . . . and cool the mercury-lifts to make them descend . . . You, though, are confused by Oric's southern magnetic pole, which reverses your compass . . . so, I suppose you would claim to be going west, then south . . . but you would still be following my directions."

He chuckles, and the image fades as the Flame Drake thrusts his droid away, going west according to your micro-compass.

If you wish to follow him, turn to **18**.

If you would prefer to follow the causeway going south, according to your micro-compass, turn to **169**.

288

After much pushing and shoving, you finally hitch a lift on the back of an unsuspecting maintenance robotron, which carries you through the crowds, back to the Space Trucker. You are relieved to find the Battledroid safe and fully recharged. Place your laser-banks on maximum.

Your pilot glances wearily back at you, shakes his head, then mumbles, "Prepare for light-speed engagement." Turn to **14**.

289

As you propel the Battledroid to the right of the Robo-Mutant, the skulking creature hisses in frustration. With the

Battledroid so close, the Robo-Mutant cannot find the room to swing the flickering tips of its laser whips against your hull. It squirms spasmodically in its attempts to strike you with the lashing tongues. (Range = 50m)

ROBO-MUTANT: Attack = 8 Defence = 7 Absorption = 2 Laser Reserves = 13 (Gain Bonus for Laser Port) (Immune to Rotary Laser-Bomb Launcher)

If you defeat the Robo-Mutant, you exit from the cave through a small, sliding portal in its southern wall. Turn to **68**.

290

You guide the Battledroid onward, scouring the swirling fog of the Fentusian Gulf for the crimson surface of Oric. Make a special note of *all* the characteristics of the Battledroid, and all the Items on your Status Chart, as your status at this point in the adventure may affect your quest later on.

If you have Satellite-Informed Radar Scan, turn to **182**.

If you do not, turn to **88**.

291

The Ice Jet causes the mercury in the glass disc to contract, and the platform descends smoothly into a vertical shaft. A portal slides shut above you. The shaft is perfectly carved and spotlessly painted white, and is bathed in a yellow light. The machinery of the mercury-lift is so fine that it gives no sign as to whether you are moving up or down, or indeed if you are moving at all. Only your depth gauge registers your slow descent into Oric.

After several minutes, a magnificent white marble tubeway suddenly rises up before you, and the mercury-lift halts at its mouth. The Battledroid is now deep in the heart of Oric. Turn to **68**.

292

Suddenly, a Mutant-Spore plummets through the scarlet mist above you. The huge glass orb is crammed with the slimy, sickly body of a Flesh Mutant, its wet eyes pressed hideously against the capsule. Maldraggon has cast these foul creatures throughout the galaxies, and this one seems somehow to have sensed your mission.

If you wish to attack the Mutant-Spore, turn to **137**.

If you wish to engage photon-boost and flee to the SpaceDrome, turn to **200**.

293

You touch the glowing info-panel and, with a hiss, your contoured pilot couch carries you down though the Battledroid until you emerge behind the controls of the Manually-Operated Shuttle. Activating the micro-computer and priming the laser-banks, you roll your hand over the control sphere and the Shuttle disengages.

The ornate Wolf Tower seems much larger through the curved screen of the Shuttle, as you dart into the tunnel to your left. The passageway is eerily lit by candles, and shadows dance across its walls. After several minutes, you see light streaming through a grill above you. Guiding the Shuttle up, you see a vertical shaft disappearing into the distance.

If you wish to attempt to remove the grill and ascend the shaft, turn to **25**.

If you would prefer to continue along the tunnel, turn to **231**.

294

Add 2 to your Pilot Skill. The Battledroid grazes the sides of a large black iron tubeway, illuminated by fluorescent wires, as it descends into the ground. The Securi-Pod has all blast-shutters lowered as it travels a pre-computed auto-pilot route, so its Rockworm occupants remain unaware of your presence. You follow the sluggish craft for several kilometres, until the tubeway suddenly expands, allowing you to guide the Battledroid upright, and – if you choose – select a new movement mode. Turn to **99**.

295

You pass your hand over the bio-reader engaging the Satellite-Informed Radar Scan's short-range search. After several seconds, it prints up a computer-generated image, showing a long line of slow-moving, heavily built four-legged beasts. You depress the Image Enhancer switch, and the picture moves in to close-up.

The beasts have skin-like plate armour, and huge spikes run along their powerful backs and long tails. Sharp silver tusks protrude from their long snouts, and their eyes seem permanently covered by a milky-skinned lid. All have Fire and Ice Jet work facilities strapped to their backs.

They are mounted by small humanoid creatures, their limbs only distinguishable by their tubular gold armour. They clasp the backs of their mounts with thick claws, and stare about them with enormous, sorrowful sapphire eyes. Your computer narrates: "Three kilometres to the south, according to my micro-compass, a convoy of Lava Beasts driven by their Flame Drake masters, their saddlebags full, move away from the Battledroid at 8.5 kilometres per hour."

*If you wish to follow the Lava Beast convoy, turn to **162**.*

*If you wish to head north-east according to your micro-compass, turn to **275**.*

*If you wish to head east according to your micro-compass, turn to **208**.*

296

The protoplastic air-lock stretches, breaks, then instantly reseals itself as the Battledroid emerges into the chamber. There is a sudden flash of white light and great bolts of electrical energy stream from your hover jets. Roll one dice and deduct the score from your laser reserves. Turn to **120**.

297

The Trucker swoops down through dense white cloud, and your pilot guides his ship through the protoplastic bubble that seals the SpaceDrome of a planet identified by your computer as Gypsum-2. The Drome is hectic and dirty, crowded with bustling robotrons, merchants hawking their wares, and the abandoned bodies of broken-down droids.

If you wish to remain in the Battledroid while the Trucker refuels, turn to **151**.

If you wish to leave the safety of your control turret and venture into the crowded SpaceDrome on foot, turn to **238**.

298

You come to a third portal, which blocks the end of the tubeway as it descends back into the rock. The portal is identical to the previous two, except for the number 25, engraved at its centre.

If you wish to insert the crystal with a diamond at its centre, turn to **128**.

If you wish to insert the crystal with a gold coin at its centre, turn to **192**.

If you wish to insert the crystal with a silver coin at its centre, turn to **44**.

If you wish to insert the Battledroid's Standard Investigation Probe into the crystal-receiver, turn to **181**.

299

The Battledroid's computer suddenly bursts into life and, imitating your voice-pattern, announces: "I am picking up a Caluphexian distress signal which, according to my micro-compass, emanates from the north. It is not stationary, however, but moves rapidly in small circles. Most curious."

If you wish to head towards the distress signal, north according to your micro-compass, turn to **2**.

If you wish to head south according to your micro-compass, turn to **208**.

If you wish to head north according to your micro-compass, but engage Hover mode and head out over the lava-lake, to avoid the distress signal, turn to **34**.

If you wish to head south-west according to your micro-compass, turn to **77**.

If you wish to head south-east according to your micro-compass, turn to **48**.

300

Your Craft Master stares silently in astonishment at you, as you explain your quest. "This is madness!" he splutters through his bedraggled beard when you have finished. "But it is a madness that pleases my heart. Take these gifts, which might help you with your quest, and contact me again if you ever need my aged mind to guide you. May the Raths go with you."

He draws two objects from the folds of his heavy white cloak and places them gently in the Shuttle's Matter Receptacle.

You nod your heartfelt thanks and steer the Shuttle quickly back along the tubeway. Turn to **103**.

301

To your relief, the shaft ends in an immense glass-walled tubeway heading north. The tubeway's disuse is shown by the cobwebs stretching wearily across it, but it is fully 300 metres across, allowing you to guide the Battledroid comfortably along it.

After 100 metres, the tubeway emerges in a large chamber, its walls lined with great iron plates. At its centre stands a hulking security droid, its laser-banks obviously exhausted years ago. The droid has a Laser Mirror hanging from its central facility socket. This facility adds 3 to your defence capacity, but weighs 4 tonnes. You may take this facility providing your total weight does not exceed 60 tonnes. If you wish, you may abandon one or more of your facilities in exchange for the Laser Mirror. (Attach the Laser Mirror and note its weight on your Status Chart. Adjust your total weight and defence capacity accordingly.)

A tubeway continues south from the chamber; turn to **228**.

302

Rather than pressing home its laser attack, the Scout-Wasp swoops down and clasps the Battledroid's head in its massive talons. There is a sudden energy-loss, and the Battledroid fails to respond to your desperate handling of its controls. You are plunged into darkness as all your lighting fails. The Scout-Wasp swoops down towards Oric, its prey dangling helplessly from its claws. Turn to **159**.

303

Reclining in the Battledroid's contoured pilot-couch, you watch in awe as the huge Black Widow Spider Droid fills the sky, ascending from its perch amidst the mists above the Wolf Tower. Two of its segmented legs lock into the shimmering red laser-rails that sweep towards Zzyus, and its other six legs trail behind it, blasting the Black Widow along with the thrust from their powerful engines.

As the Spider Droid soars into the sky, your computer informs you that it has locked into Emperor Vizo Rath's bio-pattern, and he is within transporter range. There is, though, a separate life-form close by him and the computer is unable to accurately separate their two co-ordinates.

You were never permitted to use the Battledroid's highly dangerous Matter Transporter during your apprenticeship. Can you risk transporting a hostile creature into your turret if you mishandle the Transporter controls? Your computer prints up the co-ordinates 213 and 231.

If you wish to tap 213 into the Matter Transporter, turn to **118**.

If you wish to tap 231 into the Matter Transporter, turn to **152**.

If you wish to attack the Spider Droid, turn to **62**.

If you wish to wait and watch the Spider Droid, turn to **212**.

304

As you thrust the Battledroid beneath the Viper-Coaster, the Rockworm guard snatches his arm up to his mouth and shouts an unheard order into his wrist-communicator. As you pass over the force-gate, he thrusts his gnarled claw into the bio-reader and dazzling blue force-beams shoot up from the roadway. The Viper-Coaster is shielded by the Battledroid's massive hull, which takes the full force of the electric rays. Roll one dice and deduct the score from your laser-reserves.

You guide the shuddering Battledroid on to the roadway beyond, and the force-gate rises up behind you. Turn to **110**.

305

The shaft eventually emerges in a cavernous chamber, its stippled steel walls decorated with ornate engravings depicting various droid battles. As you enter the chamber, your compass swings around to give a completely reversed reading, as if affected by some mighty underground magnet. All directions will be given according to your micro-compass.

At the centre of the chamber, a 10-metre tall robotron runs wildly in circles, screaming shrilly. Its work facilities flap frantically and its eyes have popped out on springs, bobbing wildly. The Battledroid's gyro-sensors hiss as you land several metres from the malfunctioning droid.

If you wish to attack the robotron, turn to **250**.

If you wish to investigate the robotron, turn to **164**.

306

A terrible droning suddenly fills your ears, and two Fentusian Limpet Droids rise up from the mists of the gulf. These black spheres, driven by the fluttering of tiny, sticky wings, seem alive, like hideous metal insects. Sensing your presence, they hurtle into the Battledroid, digging their barbed claws into your turret, centimetres from your face. The Limpet Droids' thin jointed legs spasmodically paw the air before jerkily reaching up to detach their own safety caps, priming themselves for explosion. You must remove them before they detonate.

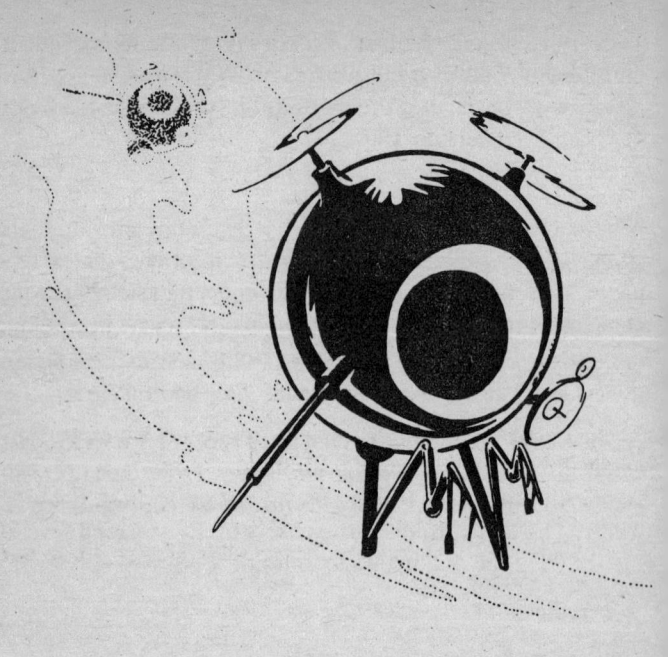

If you have and wish to use the Manually-Operated Shuttle, turn to **33**.

If you have and wish to use the Negative-Ion Flame Thrower, turn to **135**.

If you have and wish to use the Automated Claw, turn to **227**.

If you have none of these facilities, or do not wish to use any of them, turn to **202**.

307

Using its data from the Oric Mines Security Files, the computer prints up a diagram of the mercury-lift. A long glass column descends below the platform, containing the mercury, which rises from a great bulb built into the rock. When the mercury is heated, the platform rises, carrying its passenger up into the Lairs of the Lava Beasts. When it is cooled, the mercury contracts, and the platform descends into the heart of Oric. Turn back to **150**.

308

Engaging Hover, you guide the Battledroid down on to its belly, and thrust it headfirst into the Trucker cargo-bay. Great lengths of webbing, rope and chain hang down from the bay's ceiling, its floor is littered with dust and crumpled leaves, and a heavy scent penetrates your control turret.

As the Battledroid comes to rest, the Trucker pilot strolls past along the cargo-bay's footbridge, waves lazily towards you, and steps into the air-shuttle leading to his control-helm.

*Note down that you are travelling on Space Trucker Alpha, and turn to **127**.*

309

The Battledroid's exterior temperature gauges rise dramatically as you progress along the passageway, and despite the control turret's air-cooling systems, sweat breaks from your brow.

You emerge in a massive cavern, its walls glowing crimson and dripping with molten lava. The entire floor of the chamber is a mass of shifting, seething white-hot lava, and its heat blisters the Battledroid's laser-pipes. Deduct 2 from your laser-reserves.

The whole cavern swarms with the muscular frames of Lava Beasts, from four metre long babies to fully mature adults, wallowing in the scorching liquid. Their eyes, covered with a milky lid on Oric's surface, blaze red within the lair of the Lava Beasts. One of the largest creatures, with a tiny Flame

Drake perched on its spiked back, looks up at you, snorts out a cloud of steam, and launches into its fire-breathing attack.

If you have the AnthraSun, and wish to open its casket, turn to **195**.

If you do not, turn to **60**.

310

The Battledroid's computer taps into the Space Fighter's security records, and announces: "Fentusian Special Operations Blimp: Security Code: MD-SOB 246: Landing Code: Exceptional."

The pilot apologises, and raises his left hand in a grotesque Fentusian salute. The Intercom message fades and a crystal impregnated with thousands of tiny numbers emerges from your Matter Transporter. Note down "Security Crystal" on your Items list and turn to **94**.

311

The Battledroid lands safely on the central platform of the SpaceDrome Docking Hangar, and you gaze about you in wonder. The central platform is crafted from polished white marble, and is fully six kilometres across. To the south, bridges crafted from blazing light stretch across to the mouths of spiralling tubeways, and the portals of great spherical chambers. To the north, 800-metre long Dragon-Class Space Truckers rest in their laser-docks, great bays of flickering laser-energy stretching out from transparent blast screens. The marble platform rests at the centre of a great blue lake of laser beams, the SpaceDrome's energy bay, which shimmers as a gust of air blows from a Docking Portal closing in the distance. This breathtaking spectacle is enclosed in the huge glass dome which rises into the sky, casting aside Anthracitex-9's ragged cloak of scarlet cloud.

*If you have a Drome Master's golden bubble, turn to **284**.*

*If you have a Drome Master's silver bubble, turn to **180**.*

*If you have neither, turn to **100**.*

312

The Battledroid crashes into the far side of the chamber, but finds no exit. Bubbles shoot out from the gyro-sensors as they seek to keep the control tower upright, and liquid squirts into your turret from ruptured filters. Your life-support displays flash at zero, and you can't quite catch your breath. The Battledroid sinks limply down into its water-filled tomb. Your mission is over.

313

The gold crystal evaporates from the Matter Holder and appears at the old man's feet. Turn to **15**.

314

The passage's black walls, lit with veins of fluorescent wire, suddenly become transparent as the tubeway swoops out along the ceiling of a huge Space Hangar, the SpaceDrome's Holding Bay. Far below you, a 400-metre long Space-Cruiser rests on its battered belly, bathed by the eerie light of the laser-dock in which it is suspended. The golden hawk emblem daubed on its side identifies it as a captured Space-pirate Cruiser.

The tubeway emerges in a large globe hanging at the centre of the Hangar. From it, three tubeways run out of the Holding Bay.

If you wish to go north, turn to **252**.

If you wish to go west, turn to **142**.

If you wish to go south, turn to **214**.

315

The tubeway sinks back into the rock, and descends for about 100 metres before dividing into two branches, one of which is blocked by a dull grey portal. Emblazoned on the portal is a crimson orb, surrounded by a flaming circle, which seems to actually flicker and give off heat.

If you have the Droid Master's Symbol and wish to insert it in the Battledroid's Matter Transporter, turn to **230**.

If you do not, you must travel along the second branch of the tubeway, turn to **115**.

316

You are led, under arrest, along the roadway, until it widens out into a huge avenue made of steel, congested with thousands of tiny craft. They swoop aside as the massive Battledroid is guided along by your scowling Rockworm escort. You appear to be heading for the distant SpaceDrome. Turn to **54**.

317

You manoeuvre the Battledroid down on to a grey causeway of solidified lava, which cuts through a crimson sea of molten lava. The Battledroid's exterior temperature gauges rise rapidly, and its paint is blistered by the heat generated by this strange planet. A heat haze dances lazily across the lava lake as it bubbles and boils. Add 2 to your pilot skill and turn to **246**.

318

The roadway continues for two kilometres before rising up a steep incline, at the top of which is an enormous bronze portal, decorated with an engraving of a blazing circle around a globe. Sparks of electricity seem to spring from the en-

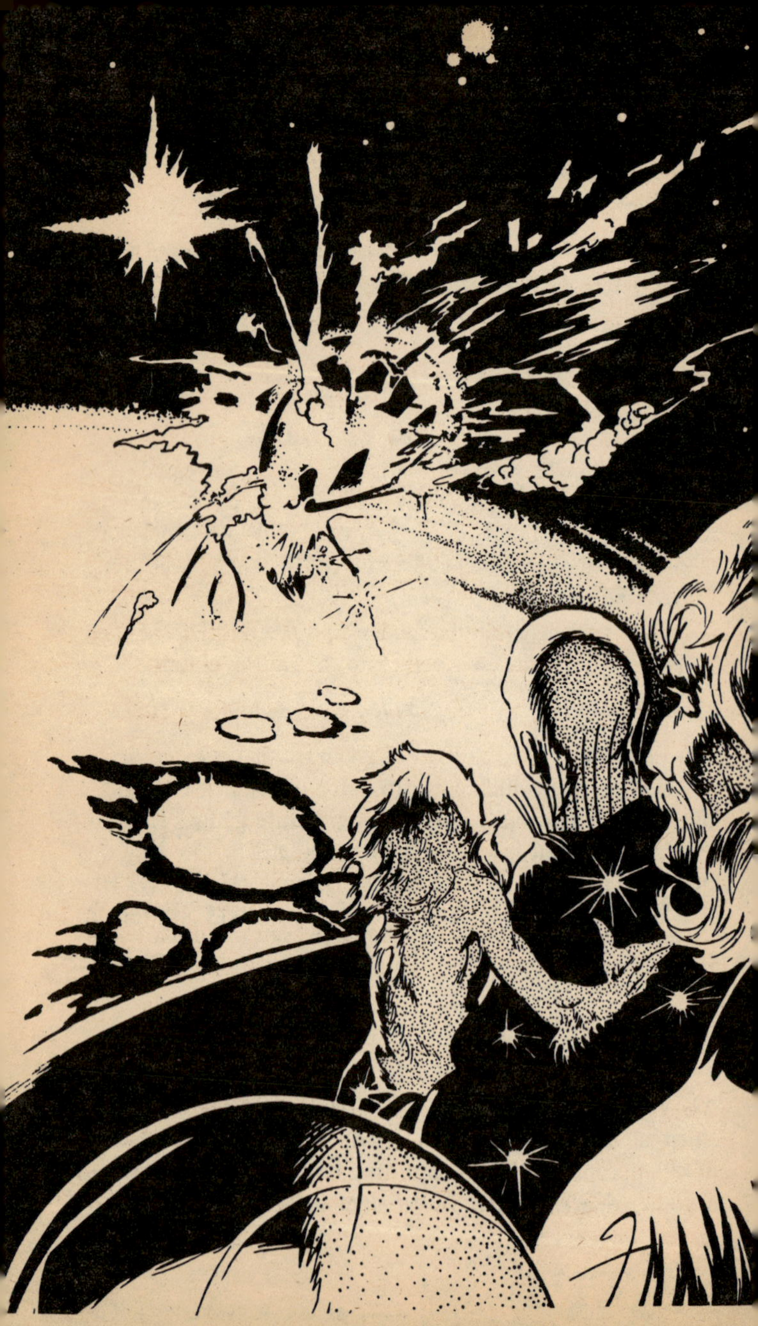

graving, and as you guide the Battledroid forward, the two halves of the portal slide open without a sound.

If you wish to head down the tunnel beneath the portal, turn to **305**.

If you wish to investigate the wide avenue which heads north according to your micro-compass, into the centre of the Metropolis, turn to **178**.

319

The Trucker pilot is unwilling to engage light-speed in the poorly charted gulf, and for a long, lonely day you drift through its silent mists. Finally, the pilot turns to you and says: "This is as far as I go. Oric is not far off. Good luck!"

He activates the jettison bio-reader, and the Battledroid slips slowly from the Trucker's belly into the murky clouds.

Shade in one day on your Status Chart, and turn to **108**.

320

The laser-banks of the Black Widow Spider Droid explode with a deafening report, releasing an ever-expanding ball of white-hot gas. The remains of the huge craft tumble towards the crimson surface of Oric, its metallic legs trailing lifelessly behind.

Vizo Rath, Overseer of Caluphex, clutches your arm, a delighted gleam illuminating his wild eyes, and chuckles at your famous victory. Gan Tamil-Rath, last of the Droid Masters, scampers up the robes of his Soul-Server, who whispers: "Without Maldraggon and Violwart to guide them, the Fentusians have no heart for war. They will soon give up their evil crusade. You have saved the galaxies, Battledroid Master."

Staring through the Battledroid's viewing screen, you watch the burning husk of the Spider Droid plummet through the bubbling surface of Oric's lava sea. After all these centuries, you have surely laid the evil spirit of Maldraggon to rest forever . . .

321

Roll one dice and add the score to the amount of damage sustained.

Total	Result
2–6:	No damage.
7–8:	Pilot injury: deduct 1 from life force.
9:	No damage.
10–11:	Watchdog Missile Guidance disabled until next recharge.
12:	No damage.
13–14:	Turret explosion: deduct 3 from laser reserves.
15+:	Pilot injury: Roll one dice and deduct score from life force.

322

Roll one dice and add the score to the amount of damage sustained.

Total	Result
2–6:	No damage
7–8:	Computer malfunction: Deduct 2 from computer capacity.
9:	No damage.

- 10–11: Attack facilities disrupted. Deduct 2 from attack capacity until next recharge.
- 12: No damage.
- 13–14: Defence facilities disrupted. Deduct 1 from defence capacity until next recharge.
- 15+: Roll three dice and add 10 to the total (13–28). If you have the work or attack facility with the same facility number, it is disabled until you next recharge.

Status Chart
SAMURAI-CLASS BATTLEDROID SB 246

Attack Capacity:
Defence Capacity:

Movement = SPACE | TRACKS / STRIDE | HOVER =

Laser Banks (Maximum:)

1	2	3	4	5	6	7	8	9	10	11	12	13	14	15	16	17	18	19	20	21	22	23	24	25

26	27	28	29	30	31	32	33	34	35	36	37	38	39	40	41	42	43	44	45	46	47	48	49	50

Computer Capacity: Pilot skill: 7

Time: | 1 | 2 | 3 | 4 | 5 | 6 | 7 | 8 | 9 | 10 | 11 | 12 | 13 | 14 | 15 |

Life Force: 7

Facility Number	Defence Facilities	Front Absorption	Rear Absorption	Weight

Facility Number	Attack Facilities	Range	Type	Charges	Bonus	Weight

Facility Number	Work Facilities			Weight
			TOTAL WEIGHT:	

Items   Notes

Battle Chart

Battledroid Attack Capacity: Defence Capacity: Laser Banks: Control tower damage: Internal electronics damage:	**Opponent** Attack Capacity: Defence Capacity: Absorption: Laser Banks:
Battledroid Attack Capacity: Defence Capacity: Laser Banks: Control tower damage: Internal electronics damage:	**Opponent** Attack Capacity: Defence Capacity: Absorption: Laser Banks:
Battledroid Attack Capacity: Defence Capacity: Laser Banks: Control tower damage: Internal electronics damage:	**Opponent** Attack Capacity: Defence Capacity: Absorption: Laser Banks:
Battledroid Attack Capacity: Defence Capacity: Laser Banks: Control tower damage: Internal electronics damage:	**Opponent** Attack Capacity: Defence Capacity: Absorption: Laser Banks:

Fig. 1 Front of Battledroid

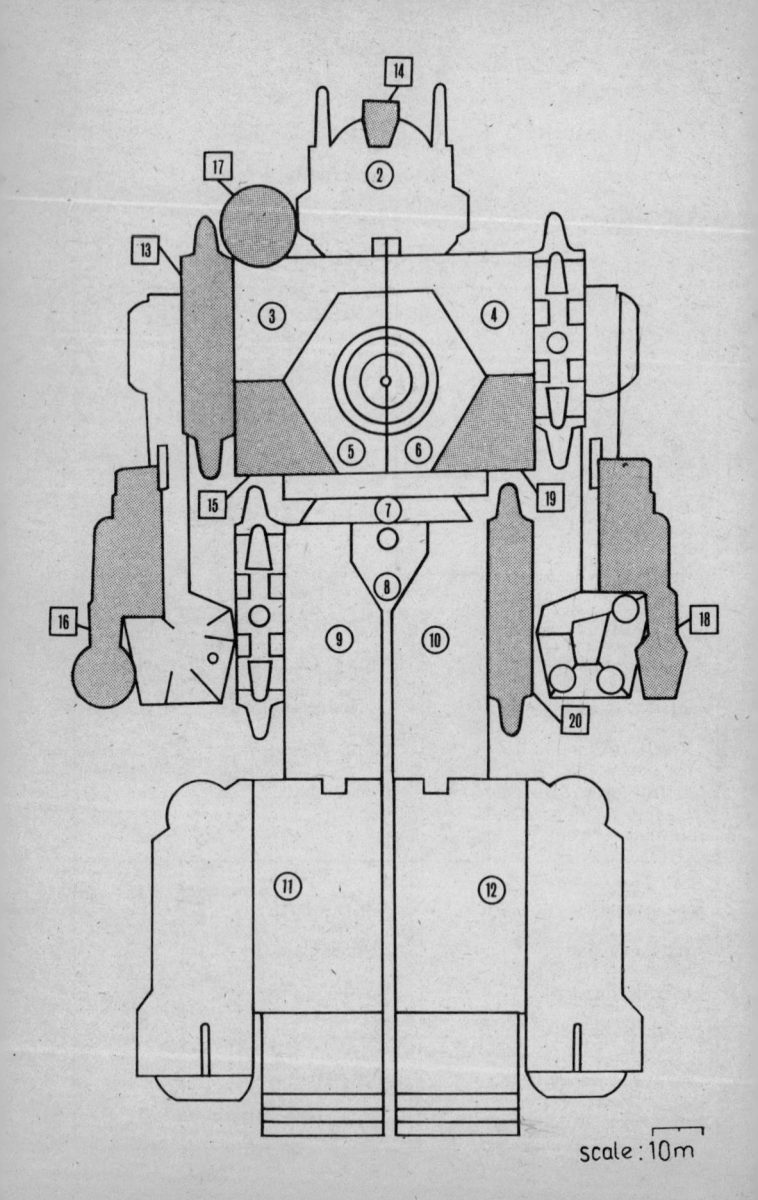

scale: 10m

Fig. 3 Facilities Available

Defence
- (2) Laser-Intercept Helm
- (3) Laserite Deflector
- (4) Laserite Deflector
- (5) Magno-Plates
- (6) Magno-Plates
- (7) Internal Electronics
- (8) Tuskquartz Energy Globe
- (9) Photonite Shielding
- (10) Photonite Shielding
- (11) Laserite Interceptor
- (12) Laserite Interceptor

Attack
- [13] Rotary Laser-bomb Launcher
- [14] Psi-Exuder
- [15] Laser Port
- [16] Sonic Punch
- [17] Negative-Ion Flame Thrower
- [18] Nuclear Gas/Water/Radiation Jet
- [19] Heat-Seeking Atomic Torpedo Launcher
- [20] Tail-Guard Disintegrator

Work
- ⟨21⟩ Satellite-Informed Radar Scan
- ⟨22⟩ Watchdog Missile Guidance System
- ⟨23⟩ Gamma-Wave Intercom
- ⟨24⟩ Automated Claw
- ⟨25⟩ Auxiliary Oxygen Supply
- ⟨26⟩ Mutant Sensory Unit
- ⟨27⟩ Manually-Operated Shuttle
- ⟨28⟩ Independent Information Probe

Fig. 2 Back of Battledroid

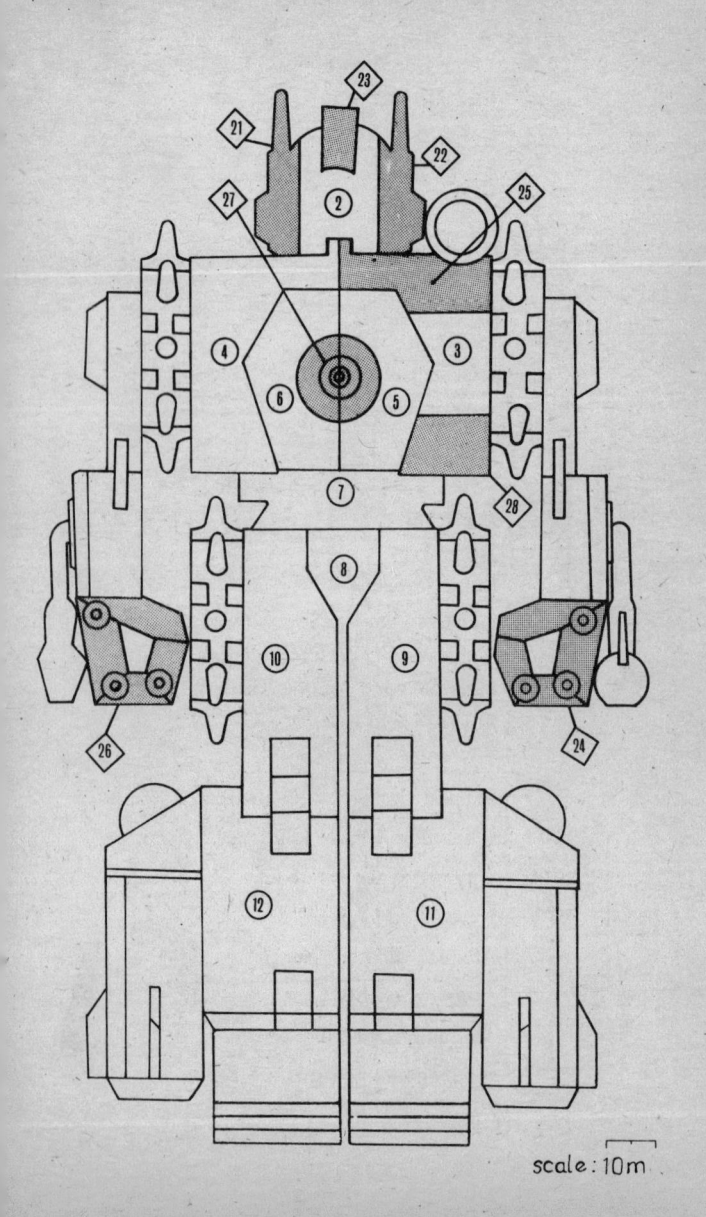

scale: 10m